Dear Reader,

Thank you for choosing "The Modern Stoic: Adapting Ancient Virtues for the Digital Age." This book is a journey into the heart of Stoicism, exploring how its timeless principles can be applied to the unique challenges of our digital era. Within these pages, you will find a blend of historical insights, practical applications, and real-life case studies that bring Stoicism into the context of our modern lives, especially in the realm of digital technology. As you embark on this journey, expect to discover ways to cultivate inner peace, resilience, and wisdom amidst the fast-paced and often overwhelming digital world. Remember, as Marcus Aurelius, a key figure in Stoicism, once said, "You have power over your mind – not outside events. Realize this, and you will find strength." Here's to finding strength and wisdom on your Stoic journey.

To: NATHANIEL

"Before beginning – plan carefully."

MARCUS TULLIUS CICERO

CIRCA· 77 BCE

Table of Contents

Introduction

Overview of Stoicism and its relevance today
The intersection of Stoicism and the digital age

Chapter 1: Origins and Evolution

Brief history of Stoicism
Key figures: Marcus Aurelius, Seneca, Epictetus
Core principles of Stoicism

Chapter 2: The Digital Dilemma

The impact of technology on modern life
Challenges: information overload, social media,
    digital distractions
Stoic perspective on managing digital
    consumption

Chapter 3: Stoic Virtues in a Digital World

Wisdom: Dealing with information and
    misinformation

Courage: Overcoming digital anxieties and
pressures
Justice: Ethics in digital interactions
Temperance: Balancing digital consumption

Chapter 4: Practical Applications

- Daily exercises for cultivating Stoicism
- Stoic responses to common digital-age
challenges
- Reflections and journaling prompts

Chapter 5: Case Studies and Real-life Applications

- Stories of individuals applying Stoicism in digital
contexts
- Analysis and insights from these stories

Conclusion: Continuing the Stoic Journey

- Resources for further exploration
Encouraging ongoing practice of Stoic principles

Introduction

In a world where change is the only constant, Stoicism stands as a beacon of stability and wisdom. This ancient philosophy, rooted in the teachings of Zeno of Citium in early 3rd century BC Greece, offers more than just a set of ideas; it provides a way of life. Stoicism, at its heart, is about understanding what we can control and letting go of what we cannot. It teaches that while we may not have power over external events, we have absolute authority over our responses, attitudes, and the values we choose to live by.

The Stoic philosophy emphasizes virtue as the highest good. The Stoics, including renowned figures like Marcus Aurelius, Seneca, and Epictetus, believed that a life well-lived was one rooted in virtues such as wisdom, courage, justice, and self-discipline. Their teachings weren't abstract musings but practical guidelines for daily living, emphasizing personal growth, inner peace, and resilience in the face of adversity.

These principles, articulated centuries ago, remain strikingly relevant. In an era defined by rapid technological advancements and societal shifts, the Stoic message of finding strength within and focusing on our internal moral compass continues to resonate deeply. As we navigate the complexities of the 21st century, Stoicism offers not just a philosophical anchor, but a practical toolkit for managing life's inevitable challenges and uncertainties.

The enduring appeal of Stoicism in the modern world can be attributed to its practicality and focus on personal resilience. In an age where uncertainty seems to be the only certainty, Stoicism provides a framework for finding steadiness and purpose. Its principles are not confined to the pages of ancient texts but are alive in the everyday challenges we face – from personal setbacks to global crises.

Stoicism teaches us to differentiate between what is within our control and what is not. This simple yet profound understanding empowers us to invest our energy wisely. In the Stoic view, our efforts are best spent on our own actions, thoughts, and feelings, rather than external events that lie beyond our influence. By cultivating a strong inner life, Stoics argue, we can maintain our equilibrium in the face of life's ebbs and flows.

Moreover, Stoicism's relevance today extends beyond individual well-being. In a world grappling with issues like climate change, political upheaval, and social injustice, Stoicism encourages us to approach these challenges with a balanced mindset. It teaches that virtue – doing the right thing for the right reason – is not just a personal goal, but a social responsibility. Stoicism, thus, becomes a call to ethical action, urging us to engage with the world in a thoughtful and principled manner.

The Stoic approach to emotions is particularly pertinent in the contemporary context. Stoicism does not advocate for the suppression of emotions but rather for understanding and managing them. This nuanced perspective helps us navigate an increasingly complex emotional landscape, where reactions are often amplified by the immediacy and intensity of digital interactions.

In essence, the principles of Stoicism provide a compass for navigating the modern world. They offer a way to cultivate personal strength, moral integrity, and emotional intelligence – qualities that are as essential today as they were in the times of Marcus Aurelius and Epictetus. Stoicism,

with its timeless wisdom, continues to guide us in leading more fulfilling and meaningful lives.
In the ever-evolving landscape of the digital age, where technology and virtual connections increasingly dominate our lives, the teachings of Stoicism offer a grounding perspective. This era, characterized by instant communication, social media platforms, and a deluge of information, presents unique challenges that test our mental and emotional resilience. Here, the wisdom of Stoicism is not just useful but vital, providing us with tools to navigate the complexities of this modern world.

The digital age, for all its advancements, often blurs the distinction between what is within our control and what is not. Social media can sway our emotions, news cycles can disturb our peace, and the constant connectivity can leave us feeling overwhelmed. Stoicism teaches us to draw a clear line, focusing on our internal reactions and actions, rather than getting swept away by the external digital currents. It encourages us to engage with technology mindfully, discerning what enriches our lives and what detracts from our well-being.

In this context, the Stoic virtues of wisdom, courage, justice, and temperance take on new meanings. Wisdom involves navigating the digital world with discernment, understanding the impact of our digital footprint, and choosing our online interactions thoughtfully. Courage is about standing firm in our values amidst the ever-changing trends and opinions on social media, and having the strength to disconnect when necessary for our mental health.

Justice in the digital age calls for ethical engagement online, respecting others' viewpoints while standing up against misinformation and harmful behaviors. Temperance, or moderation, becomes crucial in managing our time and attention in a world where digital distractions are always at our fingertips.

Thus, Stoicism provides a valuable lens through which to view our digital interactions. It encourages a balanced and intentional approach to technology, ensuring that we remain masters of our digital tools, rather than becoming their servants. By applying Stoic principles, we can find harmony and purpose in an age that is constantly connected, yet often disconnected from inner peace and wisdom.

Courage, as understood by the Stoics, is not just about confronting physical dangers but also about facing the challenges and pressures of the digital realm. In the context of the online world, courage manifests as the strength to uphold one's convictions in the face of online criticism, the resilience to endure the relentless pace and demands of digital life, and the bravery to disconnect when necessary. It involves the fortitude to resist the allure of constant digital engagement and the integrity to stay true to one's values amidst the ever-shifting narratives of social media.

In the digital age, where opinions are often polarized and expressed with fervor, courage is also about engaging in meaningful and respectful dialogues, standing up against cyberbullying, misinformation, and other harmful online behaviors. It's about having the courage to be an agent of positive change, using digital platforms to advocate for justice and truth, while also having the courage to admit when we are wrong and to learn from diverse perspectives.

Moreover, Stoic courage in the digital era includes the resilience to face the anxieties and insecurities that arise from our online engagements. In a world where social media often portrays idealized versions of life, it takes courage to accept our own realities, embrace our imperfections, and not fall into the trap of constant comparison. This form of courage is deeply personal, rooted in self-awareness and the pursuit of personal growth.

The Stoic principle of courage, therefore, extends far beyond the traditional notion of bravery. It encompasses a broad spectrum of behaviors and attitudes that are essential for navigating the complexities and challenges of the digital age. By embracing this virtue, we equip ourselves to interact with the digital world in a way that is not only brave but also wise, ethical, and balanced. Setting the stage for the modern Stoic involves understanding the profound implications of applying ancient wisdom to contemporary digital challenges. As we embark on this journey through the book, we will explore not just the philosophical underpinnings of Stoicism, but also its practical applications in the context of today's digitalized world. This exploration is aimed at empowering you, the reader, to navigate the complexities of the digital age with Stoic principles as your guide.

In the following chapters, we will delve into each of the Stoic virtues—wisdom, courage, justice, and temperance—and examine how they can be cultivated and applied in our daily digital interactions. We will provide practical tools and exercises to help you implement Stoic practices in your life, from mindful social media usage to managing digital distractions. These tools are designed to enhance your mental clarity, emotional resilience, and ethical engagement in the digital realm.

Furthermore, we will share inspiring stories of individuals who have successfully integrated Stoicism into their digital lives, offering real-life examples of how these ancient principles remain profoundly relevant and transformative in our modern world.

As we navigate through the chapters, remember that the journey of incorporating Stoicism into one's life is a personal and ongoing process. It is about finding balance, cultivating inner strength, and living a life of purpose and virtue in an age dominated by digital influences. By the end of this book, you will have gained not only a deeper understanding of Stoic philosophy but also practical strategies for living as a modern Stoic in the digital age.

Welcome to the journey of 'The Modern Stoic: Adapting Ancient Virtues for the Digital Age'. Let this be the beginning of a transformative path, where ancient wisdom meets modern technology, guiding you towards a more balanced, fulfilled, and meaningful life.

Chapter 1: Origins and Evolution

In the heart of ancient Greece, amidst the intellectual fervor of Athens, Stoicism took root. Founded by Zeno of Citium in the early 3rd century BC, Stoicism emerged as a practical philosophy, one deeply concerned with the art of living. Zeno, influenced by the teachings of Socrates and the Cynics, began teaching in the Stoa Poikile, the painted porch, from which 'Stoicism' derives its name.

Stoicism quickly distinguished itself with its focus on virtue and living in accordance with nature. It wasn't just a theory; it was a way of life, embracing personal ethics as the path to true happiness. The Stoics believed that a life lived virtuously, in harmony with reason and nature, was the highest form of existence.

As Stoicism matured, it found its way to Rome, where it flourished and evolved. Roman Stoicism, while retaining the core tenets of its Greek origins, adapted to the Roman ethos, emphasizing duty, discipline, and practical wisdom. This period saw the philosophy being practiced by slaves and emperors alike, a testament to its universal applicability and enduring appeal.

The principles of Stoicism, grounded in reason and personal ethics, offered a stark contrast to the tumultuous political and social landscapes of the time. Stoicism provided a steady moral compass, a guide for individuals seeking tranquility and purpose in a world of uncertainty. This ancient philosophy, with its profound yet practical teachings, laid the groundwork for a legacy that would endure for centuries, influencing countless individuals and shaping philosophical discourse for generations to come.

In the annals of history, Stoicism stands as a philosophy that transcended its era, leaving an indelible mark not only on its contemporaries but also on the many generations that followed. As Stoicism evolved from its Hellenistic roots, it garnered widespread appeal, particularly in the Roman Empire, where it became a guiding philosophy for leaders and citizens alike.

The enduring influence of Stoicism is evident in its impact on various historical periods and schools of thought. During the early Christian era, Stoic principles, particularly its emphasis on virtue and inner peace, resonated deeply with Christian teachings, influencing early Christian thinkers. In the Renaissance, Stoicism re-emerged as a significant intellectual influence, with its emphasis on rationality and humanism aligning well with the period's values.

As the world transitioned into the modern age, Stoicism experienced a resurgence. In the face of the complexities of modern life, the Stoic emphasis on personal resilience, ethical living, and mental fortitude found new relevance. Its practical approach to dealing with life's challenges made it particularly appealing in the realm of psychology, where Stoic concepts have been integrated into therapeutic practices, such as Cognitive Behavioral Therapy (CBT).

Moreover, Stoicism's appeal in contemporary times extends beyond academic and therapeutic spheres. It has found a place in popular culture, resonating with individuals seeking a philosophy that provides practical tools for living a fulfilled and balanced life. The digital age, with its unique challenges and stressors, has only amplified the need for a philosophy that advocates for inner peace, self-control, and rational thinking.

Thus, the journey of Stoicism, from its origins in ancient Greece to its modern-day applications, is a testament to its timeless relevance and adaptability. As we delve deeper into the lives and teachings of its key figures and core principles, it becomes evident why Stoicism continues to be a beacon of wisdom in an ever-changing world.

Marcus Aurelius - The Philosopher Emperor

Among the luminaries of Stoicism, Marcus Aurelius stands as a towering figure, embodying the principles of this philosophy not just in thought, but in action. Born into Roman nobility in 121 AD, Marcus Aurelius ascended to the Roman throne, becoming one of the most respected emperors in Roman history. His reign was marked by wisdom and justice, but it was his personal writings, later compiled as "Meditations," that cemented his legacy as a Stoic philosopher.

"Meditations," written during military campaigns and the quiet solitude of his study, offers a rare glimpse into the inner workings of a Stoic mind.

These writings were not meant for publication; they were Marcus's personal reflections, his way of practicing Stoicism in the tumult of his responsibilities as emperor. In these pages, he wrestled with concepts of fate, virtue, and the nature of the mind, offering insights that are strikingly relevant even today.

Marcus Aurelius's Stoicism was grounded in humility and self-discipline. He saw power not as a privilege, but as a duty, a means to serve the greater good. His reflections reveal a man deeply committed to the Stoic virtues of wisdom, justice, courage, and temperance. He emphasized the importance of rationality and self-control, recognizing the impermanence of life and the value of living in harmony with nature.

His teachings in "Meditations" resonate with a profound understanding of the human condition. He speaks of the need to face life's challenges with equanimity, to treat others with compassion and respect, and to find contentment in fulfilling one's duties. Marcus Aurelius, through his life and words, exemplifies the ideal Stoic, one who finds strength and tranquility not in the trappings of power, but in the steadfast adherence to virtue.

Seneca - The Statesman and Playwright

Lucius Annaeus Seneca, commonly known as Seneca, offers a different yet equally profound perspective on Stoicism. Born in Corduba (now Córdoba, Spain) in 4 BC, Seneca rose to prominence in Rome as a statesman, dramatist, and philosopher. His life, marked by political intrigue and personal tragedy, provides a backdrop to his extensive body of work, which includes philosophical essays, letters, and tragedies.

Seneca's contributions to Stoicism are found primarily in his essays and the Moral Letters to Lucilius. These writings are remarkable for their practicality and accessibility. Seneca's style is direct and often intensely personal, reflecting his belief that philosophy should be a practice, not just a theory. He tackled topics ranging from grief and happiness to wealth and poverty, always through the lens of Stoic philosophy.

His philosophy centers around the idea of living in accordance with nature and reason. He emphasized the transitory nature of external goods and the importance of inner tranquility. Unlike some of his Stoic predecessors, Seneca often explored the complexities of emotions, advocating for a balance where emotions are acknowledged but not allowed to dominate reason.

Seneca's Stoicism is particularly relevant in the context of his political career. He served as an advisor to Emperor Nero, a role that tested his philosophical convictions. Despite the challenges and moral dilemmas he faced, Seneca endeavored to live by his Stoic principles, advocating for clemency and rational governance.

In his tragedies, Seneca explored themes of passion, power, and moral struggle, offering a dramatic illustration of Stoic principles in conflict with human frailties. His works not only contribute to our understanding of Stoicism but also offer timeless insights into the human condition, reflecting the enduring relevance of Stoic wisdom in navigating the complexities of life.

Epictetus - The Enslaved Philosopher

Epictetus, born into slavery around 50 AD, stands as a testament to the universal applicability of

Stoic philosophy. His journey from a slave in Rome to a revered Stoic teacher in Greece is a story of resilience and the transformative power of philosophy. Unlike Marcus Aurelius, who penned his thoughts in a position of power, or Seneca, who navigated the complex corridors of politics, Epictetus experienced Stoicism from the standpoint of servitude and later, as a freedman.

The core of Epictetus's teaching is encapsulated in the opening line of his handbook, the Enchiridion: "Some things are in our control and others not." This simple dichotomy forms the backbone of his philosophy. Epictetus emphasized the significance of focusing on one's own actions and attitudes, as these are within the realm of one's control, while accepting the external events that cannot be changed.

Epictetus's lectures, compiled by his student Arrian into the Discourses, are practical, direct, and often blunt. They reflect his belief that philosophy should be lived, not just studied. He taught that freedom and happiness are attainable by anyone, regardless of their external circumstances, through the disciplined pursuit of wisdom, self-control, and inner peace.

His teachings often revolved around the idea of self-examination and personal accountability. Epictetus urged his students to scrutinize their impressions and judgments, emphasizing that it is not events themselves that disturb people, but their judgments about those events. This perspective is especially powerful in its application to overcoming adversity and maintaining tranquility in the face of life's trials.

Epictetus's life and teachings demonstrate that Stoicism is not just a philosophy for the elite or the learned, but a practical guide for anyone seeking to live a virtuous and meaningful life. His emphasis on inner freedom and the power of personal choice continues to inspire and guide people from all walks of life in their quest for a fulfilling existence.

The Four Cardinal Virtues

The core of Stoic philosophy rests upon four cardinal virtues: wisdom, courage, justice, and temperance. These virtues form the foundation of Stoic ethics and provide a framework for living a good and meaningful life. In Stoicism, virtue is not an abstract concept but a practical guide to daily living, offering a path to true happiness and fulfillment.

Wisdom, in the Stoic sense, is the knowledge of what is good, what is bad, and what is indifferent. It encompasses the ability to navigate complex situations with clarity and rationality, making decisions that align with our true nature and the nature of the universe. Wisdom involves not just theoretical understanding but also practical insight into how to act and respond to various circumstances in life.

Courage is not merely physical bravery but also the mental and moral strength to endure, overcome, and face fear, uncertainty, and difficulty. In Stoicism, courage means standing firm in our convictions, even in the face of adversity, and doing the right thing even when it is difficult. It is about confronting the challenges of life with resilience and determination.

Justice is central to Stoic ethics and involves the practice of fairness, kindness, and social responsibility. It is about treating others with respect and dignity, acting with integrity, and contributing to the well-being of society. In

Stoicism, justice extends beyond legal obligations to encompass a moral duty to do what is right, not only for oneself but for others as well.

Temperance, or self-control, is the virtue of moderation. It involves regulating our desires and impulses, ensuring that our actions are in harmony with our best selves. Temperance is about finding balance, whether it be in our physical appetites, emotions, or ambitions, and avoiding excess and extremes.

These virtues are not isolated traits but are interdependent and interconnected. They work together, guiding us in our journey towards a Stoic life. By cultivating these virtues, Stoics believe we can achieve a state of eudaimonia, a life of flourishing and true happiness. This pursuit of virtue is not just a personal endeavor but a universal one, applicable to all, regardless of life's external circumstances.

Understanding What We Can Control

A fundamental aspect of Stoic philosophy is the distinction between what is within our control and what is not. This principle is not just a theoretical concept but a practical tool for living with tranquility and effectiveness. By focusing on what we can control and accepting what we cannot, we free ourselves from unnecessary distress and are empowered to act more effectively.

In Stoicism, what we can control are our own actions, reactions, and judgments. This includes our thoughts, feelings, decisions, and behaviors. Epictetus famously stated, "It's not what happens to you, but how you react to it that matters." This encapsulates the Stoic approach to focusing on our internal responses rather than external events. We might not have control over the actions of others, the weather, or unforeseen events, but we do have control over how we choose to respond to these situations.

Understanding and applying this principle involves a shift in perspective. It requires us to examine our reactions to challenges and to question whether our distress is caused by the event itself or by our interpretation of it. By changing our focus from external events to our internal responses, we gain a sense of empowerment and clarity.

This Stoic practice is particularly relevant in the face of adversity or in situations where our environment is beyond our control. Instead of expending energy on frustration or worry about uncontrollable aspects, Stoicism teaches us to direct our efforts towards our own responses and actions, which are within our power to change.

In daily life, this can mean choosing to respond to a difficult situation with patience rather than anger, or deciding to focus on positive actions rather than dwelling on negative circumstances. By consistently practicing this principle, we cultivate a mindset that is more resilient, calm, and effective, enabling us to navigate life's challenges with a greater sense of peace and purpose.

The Path to Inner Peace

Stoicism offers a profound approach to achieving inner peace, emphasizing the cultivation of a tranquil mind amidst life's inevitable turmoil. This pursuit of tranquility is not about detaching from the world or suppressing emotions; instead, it is about developing a state of inner harmony and resilience that enables us to face life's challenges with equanimity.

The Stoic path to inner peace begins with the understanding that our emotions are largely the product of our judgments and beliefs. Stoics argue that it is not external events that disturb us, but our opinions about these events. By reassessing and reshaping our judgments, we can alter our emotional responses. This process involves practicing mindfulness and self-awareness, observing our thoughts and reactions without immediate judgment or reaction.

Another key aspect of achieving inner peace in Stoicism is the practice of focusing on the present moment. Stoics emphasize the importance of living in the 'here and now,' avoiding excessive worry about the future or regret about the past. Marcus Aurelius advised, "Do not let the future disturb you. You will meet it, if you have to, with the same weapons of reason which today arm you against the present."

Moreover, Stoicism advocates for the acceptance of what cannot be changed. This acceptance is not a passive resignation but an active engagement with reality as it is. It involves recognizing the limits of our power and surrendering to the natural flow of life, understanding that some things are beyond our control.

Practicing gratitude is also a vital component of Stoic tranquility. Stoics encourage us to appreciate what we have, focusing on the positives in our life, rather than longing for what we lack. This perspective fosters contentment and a sense of abundance, even in simple living.

By integrating these practices into our daily lives, we cultivate a mindset that is not easily swayed by external circumstances. We develop the ability to remain calm and centered, maintaining our inner peace even in the face of life's challenges. This Stoic tranquility is not a fleeting state but a lasting condition of the soul, a deep-seated serenity that enriches our lives and enables us to live with dignity, purpose, and grace.

Living in Accordance with Nature

A central tenet of Stoicism is the concept of living in accordance with nature. This principle extends beyond an environmental or ecological understanding; it encompasses aligning oneself with the rational and moral order of the universe. The Stoics believed that the universe is governed by a divine reason, or 'logos', and that human beings, as rational creatures, are part of this natural order.

Living in accordance with nature means living in harmony with one's true self and the world around us. It involves recognizing and accepting our place in the greater scheme of things, understanding that we are part of a vast interconnected system. This perspective encourages a sense of humility and fosters an attitude of respect towards others and the world.

For the Stoics, living in accordance with nature also meant living virtuously, as virtue was considered the highest expression of human nature. This involves embracing the Stoic virtues of wisdom, courage, justice, and temperance, and applying them in our daily lives. By doing so, we align our actions with the rational order of the universe, leading to a fulfilling and meaningful life.

This Stoic principle also emphasizes the importance of reason and rational thought. Stoics believed that reason is what distinguishes humans from other animals, and it should guide our actions and decisions. By using reason, we can discern the proper course of action in any situation, make wise choices, and respond to life's challenges with clarity and composure.

Furthermore, living in accordance with nature involves accepting the events that occur in the natural world, including those that are beyond our control. This acceptance does not imply passivity; rather, it is an acknowledgment of the limits of our power and an understanding that some things are part of the natural course of life.

By striving to live in accordance with nature, we cultivate a life that is in harmony with the world and ourselves. This approach encourages us to live authentically, make reasoned choices, and find contentment in our place within the natural order of the universe. It is a path that leads to a profound sense of peace and a deep connection with the world around us.

Stoicism and the Community

The final core principle of Stoicism involves the role of the individual within the community and society at large. Stoicism teaches that each person is part of a larger whole, a member of the human community, and thus has responsibilities towards others. This perspective is grounded in the concept of cosmopolitanism, the idea that all human beings, regardless of their background, are citizens of a single, global community.

In Stoicism, the virtue of justice is closely tied to our interactions with others and our role in society. Justice, from a Stoic perspective, is not merely about legal or formal fairness but encompasses a broader moral obligation to treat others with dignity, respect, and kindness. It involves acting with integrity and working towards the common good. Stoics believe that by doing our part to contribute positively to society, we live in accordance with nature and fulfill our role as rational beings.

This communal aspect of Stoicism also emphasizes empathy and understanding. Stoics advocate for seeing the world from others' perspectives, understanding that all people have their own struggles and journeys. This empathetic approach fosters a sense of connection and encourages us to act in ways that are beneficial not only for ourselves but for others as well.

Moreover, Stoicism encourages active engagement in public life and community affairs. Stoics like Marcus Aurelius and Seneca were deeply involved in the political and social issues of their time. They believed that it was important to use one's influence and abilities for the betterment of society. This does not necessarily mean holding public office; it can be as simple as being a responsible and engaged member of one's community, contributing in whatever way possible.

Stoicism, therefore, is not a philosophy of isolation or self-absorption. It is a guide for living a life that is not only personally fulfilling but also socially responsible. It teaches us to balance our own needs and desires with our duties and responsibilities towards others. By embracing the Stoic principles of wisdom, courage, justice, and temperance, we can lead lives that are not only virtuous but also contribute to the greater good of humanity, fostering a world that is more just, compassionate, and harmonious.

Chapter 2: The Digital Dilemma

In the panorama of human history, the rapid ascent of technology stands as a defining feature of the modern era. From the smartphones in our pockets to the pervasive presence of the internet, technology has seamlessly woven itself into the fabric of daily life. Its integration is so profound that it shapes not only how we communicate and work but also how we think, learn, and entertain ourselves.

The dawn of the digital age brought with it an unparalleled access to information and a connectivity that transcends geographical boundaries. Today, we can instantly reach out to someone across the globe, access vast libraries of knowledge with a few clicks, and automate tasks that once required extensive human effort. This digital revolution has transformed mundane aspects of our lives, making many tasks more efficient and accessible.

However, as we marvel at these technological advancements, it's crucial to acknowledge the depth of their influence. Technology is no longer a mere tool; it has become a constant companion, an integral part of our waking lives. Our days begin and end with digital interactions, from morning alarms on our smartphones to evening scrolls through social media.

The ubiquity of technology presents a unique scenario in human evolution, where our environment is increasingly digital. This new landscape offers immense possibilities, but it also raises important questions about how we interact with technology and how it affects our well-being, relationships, and perception of the world. As we navigate this digital terrain, the wisdom of Stoicism can provide valuable insights into balancing the benefits of technology with the need for a meaningful and virtuous life.

The benefits and transformations brought about by technology in our modern life are both profound and far-reaching. On a fundamental level, technology has revolutionized communication, transforming it from a process bound by time and distance into an instant, effortless exchange. This connectivity has reshaped not just personal interactions but also the global economy, education, and governance. It has enabled collaborations that span continents, democratized access to information, and given voice to those who were previously unheard.

In the realm of work, technology has introduced remarkable efficiencies and innovations. Automation and digital tools have redefined traditional occupations, created new professions, and reshaped the workplace dynamics. The rise of remote work, fueled by technological advancements, has reimagined the concept of the office, offering flexibility and challenging the traditional 9-to-5 paradigm.

Education, too, has been transformed by technology. E-learning platforms, digital textbooks, and online courses have made education more accessible, accommodating diverse learning styles and needs. Students can now access a wealth of resources and experiences that were once beyond reach, breaking down barriers to education and knowledge.

Entertainment and media consumption have also undergone a digital metamorphosis. Streaming services, social media platforms, and digital content creation have revolutionized how we consume entertainment, offering a plethora of choices at our fingertips. This shift has not only changed the way we relax and amuse ourselves but also the very nature of the content we consume, giving rise to new genres and forms of storytelling.

However, these transformations come with their own set of challenges. As technology becomes more integrated into our lives, it's essential to consider its impact on our mental health, social skills, and the quality of our interactions. The ease of access to information and connectivity, while beneficial, can also lead to information overload and a sense of disconnection from the physical world.

In this new digital era, where technology is an inescapable part of our existence, the principles of Stoicism can provide a guiding light. They offer a framework for finding balance and maintaining our humanity in a world increasingly mediated by screens and devices. As we delve deeper into the challenges posed by the digital age, we can turn to Stoic wisdom to navigate these waters with grace and equilibrium.

Information Overload

In the digital age, one of the most pervasive challenges we face is information overload. With the advent of the internet and social media, we have access to an unprecedented volume of information. News, opinions, data, and messages bombard us constantly, creating a relentless stream that can be overwhelming to process and discern.

This deluge of information presents a unique challenge to our cognitive capacities. The human brain, while remarkably adaptable, has limits in processing and retaining information. When inundated with data, we can struggle to focus, make decisions, and retain important details. This constant influx can lead to a phenomenon known as 'analysis paralysis,' where the sheer volume of information hampers our ability to make decisions or draw conclusions.

Moreover, the quality of information available online varies significantly. The ease with which content can be created and shared has led to a landscape where fact, opinion, and misinformation often coexist, making it increasingly difficult to discern truth from falsehood. This challenge is compounded by algorithms that tailor content to our perceived preferences, creating echo chambers that reinforce our beliefs and shield us from differing viewpoints.

The impact of information overload extends beyond decision-making difficulties. It can also lead to a sense of mental exhaustion and stress, as we try to navigate and make sense of the constant stream of data. The feeling of needing to stay constantly updated can create anxiety, particularly when the information pertains to global crises or issues that evoke strong emotional responses.

In this environment of incessant information, the Stoic practice of focusing on what is within our control becomes increasingly relevant. It invites us to step back and evaluate the necessity and relevance of the information we consume. By applying Stoic discernment, we can learn to navigate the digital landscape more mindfully, focusing on information that is truly beneficial and aligns with our values and goals, while letting go of the compulsion to absorb everything that comes our way. This selective engagement with digital content is not only a way to manage information overload but also a path to maintaining mental clarity and peace in the information-saturated world of the digital age.

Social Media and Its Impact

Social media, a cornerstone of modern digital life, wields a profound influence on how we perceive and interact with the world. Platforms designed to connect us with others have reshaped the landscape of communication, creating virtual communities that transcend physical boundaries. While these platforms offer unprecedented opportunities for networking, learning, and sharing, they also present significant challenges that impact our mental and emotional well-being.

One of the most notable effects of social media is its impact on our perceptions and self-image. The curated nature of social media content, where users often present idealized versions of their lives, can lead to unrealistic comparisons and a sense of inadequacy. This phenomenon, known as the "compare and despair" effect, can result in feelings of envy, low self-esteem, and dissatisfaction with one's own life.

Furthermore, social media has transformed the dynamics of social interaction and communication. The immediacy and brevity of digital communication can sometimes strip away the nuance and depth of face-to-face interactions. While it enables us to maintain connections over long distances, it can also lead to a superficiality in relationships, where quantity of connections trumps the quality of engagement.

Another challenge posed by social media is the echo chamber effect, where algorithm-driven content feeds tend to reinforce existing beliefs and viewpoints, limiting exposure to diverse perspectives. This can create a polarized and insular environment, where users become entrenched in their views and less open to dialogue and understanding.

Amidst these challenges, a Stoic approach to social media involves practicing moderation and mindfulness. It encourages us to engage with these platforms intentionally, with an awareness of their impact on our mental state and worldview. Stoicism teaches us to seek inner validation rather than external approval, reminding us that true contentment comes from living in accordance with our values and virtues. By applying Stoic principles, we can use social media as a tool for positive engagement and learning, while guarding against its potential to disrupt our tranquility and sense of self.

The Lure of Digital Distractions

In the digital era, one of the most pervasive challenges is the lure of digital distractions. Our daily lives are inundated with a plethora of digital stimuli, from the constant pings of notifications to the endless scroll of social media feeds. These distractions, while seemingly innocuous, can have a profound impact on our productivity, attention span, and overall mental well-being.

The design of many digital platforms and devices is geared towards capturing and holding our attention. Features like notifications, likes, and endless content feeds exploit psychological mechanisms, creating a loop of instant gratification that can be hard to resist. This constant engagement with digital devices can fragment our attention, making it difficult to focus on tasks for extended periods and diminishing our capacity for deep, reflective thought.

The consequences of digital distractions extend beyond the loss of focus. They can lead to a sense of fragmentation, where our attention is continuously divided among multiple tasks and inputs, preventing us from fully engaging with any single activity. This state of constant partial attention can be mentally exhausting, reducing our ability to think creatively and solve problems effectively.

Additionally, the ease of access to digital entertainment and information can lead to procrastination and a delay in tackling important tasks. The immediate pleasure of engaging with digital content can overshadow the longer-term satisfaction of achieving goals and completing responsibilities.

In addressing the challenge of digital distractions, Stoicism offers valuable insights. It teaches us the importance of self-discipline and the cultivation of focus. Stoic philosophy encourages us to be mindful of our impulses and to exercise control over our reactions and attention. By adopting a Stoic approach, we can learn to prioritize our time and attention, focusing on what truly matters and aligns with our goals and values. This mindful engagement with digital technology allows us to harness its benefits while mitigating its potential to disrupt our focus and tranquility.

Stoic Approach to Digital Moderation

In confronting the digital dilemma, Stoicism provides a framework for moderation and mindful engagement with technology. The Stoic virtue of temperance, or self-control, is particularly relevant in managing our digital consumption. It teaches us to use technology intentionally, in ways that contribute positively to our lives, without allowing it to dominate our time and mental space.

The first step in practicing digital moderation is self-awareness. We must become conscious of our digital habits: the amount of time we spend online, the nature of the content we consume, and how our digital interactions affect our emotions and thoughts. This awareness allows us to make informed decisions about our technology use, rather than being driven by habit or impulse.

Stoicism also emphasizes the importance of intentionality in our actions. When engaging with digital media, we should ask ourselves: Does this activity align with my values and goals? Is it contributing to my well-being and personal growth? By being deliberate about our digital consumption, we can choose activities that are enriching and purposeful, rather than mindlessly scrolling or consuming content passively.

Another Stoic practice that can be applied to digital moderation is the concept of voluntary discomfort. This involves occasionally abstaining from digital devices or certain types of digital content, to remind ourselves that we can control our impulses and do not need constant digital stimulation. These periods of disconnection can also provide space for reflection, relaxation, and engagement with the physical world, which are essential for a balanced life.

Additionally, Stoicism teaches us to focus on what we can control. In the context of digital consumption, this means recognizing that we cannot control the vast array of content and stimuli available online, but we can control our responses to it. We can choose to disengage from content that is distressing or unproductive and focus our attention on content that is beneficial and uplifting.

By applying these Stoic principles, we can develop a balanced and mindful approach to technology. Digital moderation is not about rejecting technology altogether but about using it in a way that enhances our lives without overshadowing them. It is about finding harmony between our digital and physical worlds, ensuring that our engagement with technology is intentional, purposeful, and in line with our deeper values and aspirations.

Cultivating Digital Wisdom

In navigating the digital world, the Stoic principle of wisdom takes on a new dimension. Digital wisdom involves discerning the value and impact of digital information and interactions, making choices that reflect our highest selves. It requires us to apply critical thinking, reflection, and a deep understanding of our values to our digital engagements.

To cultivate digital wisdom, we must first develop the ability to critically assess the information we encounter online. This means not only fact-checking and considering the sources of information but also reflecting on the underlying intentions and biases that may be present.

Wisdom in the digital age calls for a discerning eye that can see beyond sensational headlines and emotionally charged content, seeking truth and depth.

Moreover, digital wisdom involves being mindful of the impact of our digital consumption on our mental and emotional state. It requires us to ask: How does engaging with certain types of content make us feel? Does it contribute to our growth and understanding, or does it leave us feeling anxious, envious, or overwhelmed? By being attuned to the emotional effects of our digital interactions, we can make more conscious choices about what we consume and how we engage online.

Stoic wisdom also extends to our digital communication. It involves being thoughtful about what we share, how we express ourselves, and the conversations we engage in. Digital wisdom calls for communication that is honest, respectful, and constructive, avoiding impulsivity and reactivity. It encourages us to use digital platforms not just for self-expression but for fostering meaningful connections and dialogue.

Additionally, applying Stoic wisdom to our digital lives means recognizing the transient nature of much of the digital world. The Stoics taught that external events and possessions are not within our control and are ultimately impermanent. This perspective can help us maintain a healthy detachment from the digital world, reminding us to find our worth and contentment from within, rather than from online validation or digital achievements.

In essence, cultivating digital wisdom is about aligning our digital habits with our deeper values and aspirations. It is about using technology not as an end in itself but as a tool for living a more informed, connected, and meaningful life. By practicing digital wisdom, we can navigate the complexities of the online world with clarity, purpose, and a sense of inner tranquility.

Building Digital Resilience

Digital resilience, a key aspect of navigating the digital age, is deeply rooted in Stoic philosophy. It involves developing the mental and emotional fortitude to face online challenges and maintain a balanced perspective in the digital realm. In Stoicism, resilience is not about avoiding difficulties but about cultivating the inner strength to overcome them.

In the context of digital resilience, this means learning to cope with the negative aspects of the digital world, such as online criticism, cyberbullying, or the pressure to conform to certain standards and trends. Stoicism teaches us to view these challenges as opportunities for growth, encouraging us to respond with reason and equanimity rather than react with emotion or impulsivity.

A Stoic approach to digital resilience also involves recognizing that our self-worth is not dependent on online validation or social media metrics. Stoicism reminds us that true value comes from living in accordance with our virtues and principles, not from external approval. By internalizing this belief, we can engage with social media and other digital platforms without being swayed by the pursuit of likes, followers, or other superficial markers of success.

Balancing our online engagement with real-world connections and activities is another crucial aspect of digital resilience. While the digital world offers many benefits, it is essential to maintain strong ties to the physical world and our immediate surroundings. This involves nurturing face-to-face relationships, engaging in physical activities, and taking time to disconnect from digital devices to enjoy the simplicity and beauty of the natural world.

Practicing mindfulness and reflection is also key to building digital resilience. Regularly taking time to reflect on our digital habits, the content we consume, and how it affects us can help us maintain a healthy perspective. Mindfulness practices, such as meditation or journaling, can be particularly effective in managing the mental and emotional impact of our digital lives.

In essence, building digital resilience is about cultivating a robust inner life that can withstand the pressures and challenges of the digital age. It involves using Stoic principles to navigate the online world with wisdom and self-control, maintaining our integrity and inner peace amidst the ever-changing digital landscape. By developing digital resilience, we can harness the benefits of technology while protecting our mental and emotional well-being.

Practicing Digital Justice

In the realm of digital interactions, the Stoic virtue of justice takes on a critical role. Digital justice involves ethical behavior, empathy, and responsible communication online. It's about treating others with respect and dignity in the digital space, just as we would in person. This virtue calls for a conscientious approach to our online presence, recognizing that our actions have real consequences in the virtual world.

One aspect of digital justice is ethical behavior. This means being honest and authentic in our digital interactions, respecting others' privacy, and not engaging in or supporting harmful online practices like cyberbullying or spreading misinformation. It's about being a responsible digital citizen, contributing positively to online communities and conversations.

Empathy is another key element of digital justice. The anonymity and distance that the digital world provides can sometimes lead us to forget that there are real people behind the screens. Practicing empathy involves trying to understand the perspectives and feelings of others online, engaging in constructive dialogues, and avoiding harsh or judgmental language.

Responsible communication is also crucial. This means sharing information thoughtfully, considering the accuracy and impact of what we post or share. It's about using our digital platforms to promote understanding and knowledge, rather than division or falsehood. In a world where digital content can spread rapidly and widely, taking responsibility for our communications is more important than ever.

Digital justice also extends to how we navigate the vast array of content and interactions available online. It involves discerning what is fair, what contributes to the greater good, and what aligns with our values. By practicing digital justice, we contribute to creating a healthier, more respectful, and more constructive digital environment.

In essence, practicing digital justice in the Stoic sense is about bringing our highest ethical standards to our digital engagements. It's about remembering our interconnectedness and our responsibilities to each other, even in the digital sphere. By applying the principles of Stoic justice to our online behavior, we can help foster a digital world that is more empathetic, honest, and respectful.

Embracing Digital Tranquility

In the Stoic journey through the digital age, the ultimate goal is to achieve a state of digital tranquility - a calm, balanced, and harmonious relationship with technology. This involves cultivating an inner peace that remains undisturbed by the turbulence of the digital world. It is about finding a middle path where we can enjoy the benefits of technology without letting it dominate our lives or disturb our mental and emotional equilibrium.

To embrace digital tranquility, we must first establish routines and boundaries for our technology use. This might involve designated times for checking emails and social media, periods of digital disconnection, and mindful practices like digital detoxes. These habits help to prevent technology from becoming an incessant distraction and allow us to be more present in our offline lives.

Another important aspect of digital tranquility is the practice of focusing on what we can control in the digital realm. This Stoic principle reminds us that while we cannot control the vast array of information and interactions online, we can control our reactions to them. We can choose to engage with digital content that is uplifting and informative and disengage from content that causes distress or distraction.

Acceptance is also key to achieving digital tranquility. This involves accepting that the digital world, like everything else, has its limitations and imperfections. It means recognizing that we won't always have the latest gadgets, keep up with every trend, or please everyone online. Acceptance allows us to interact with the digital world without becoming overly attached or affected by it.

Mindfulness is another crucial element in fostering digital tranquility. By being fully present and aware during our digital interactions, we can enjoy them more fully and avoid mindless scrolling or consumption. Mindfulness in the digital context means engaging with technology intentionally, understanding its purpose in our lives, and appreciating the moments of connection and learning it provides.

In essence, embracing digital tranquility is about using Stoic wisdom to navigate the digital world with intention and balance. It's about harnessing the benefits of technology while maintaining our inner peace, self-control, and focus on what truly matters. By cultivating digital tranquility, we can create a harmonious relationship with technology, one that enhances our lives without overshadowing our essential nature and values.

Chapter 3: Stoic Virtues in a Digital World

In the Stoic pursuit of a virtuous life, wisdom plays a crucial role, especially in the context of the digital age. This era, characterized by an abundance of information and the ease of its access, demands from us not just the consumption of content, but a discerning engagement with it. Wisdom in the digital world means navigating the vast seas of information with a critical mind and a discerning heart.

Stoicism teaches us that wisdom is not merely about acquiring knowledge; it's about understanding the nature of things, discerning what is true, what is right, and how to live well. In the digital context, this translates to an ability to sift through the vast amount of information available online, to differentiate between what is meaningful and what is superfluous, what is factual and what is fallacious.

The digital age presents us with a paradox: while we have access to more information than ever before, this abundance can often lead to confusion, misinformation, and a sense of being overwhelmed. The Stoic practice of wisdom calls for a thoughtful approach to this challenge. It involves not passively consuming whatever information comes our way but actively engaging with it, questioning its veracity, its source, and its alignment with our values.

This approach to digital information consumption is not about skepticism for skepticism's sake. Instead, it's about cultivating a balanced mindset that remains open yet critical, inquisitive yet discerning. It's about harnessing the power of information for our growth and development while remaining vigilant against its potential to mislead or distract.

As we delve deeper into the digital age, the Stoic virtue of wisdom becomes not just a tool for personal enlightenment but a shield against the pitfalls of misinformation and bias. It empowers us to navigate the digital landscape with confidence, ensuring that our engagement with information is constructive, meaningful, and aligned with our pursuit of a virtuous life.

Navigating the Information Landscape

In a world awash with data, discerning valuable information from the vast sea of content available online is a critical skill. The digital age has democratized access to knowledge, but it has also created a landscape where information is abundant and not always accurate or beneficial. Stoic wisdom in this context is not just about filtering content, but about engaging with it in a way that enriches our understanding and contributes to our personal growth.

The process of navigating this landscape requires a discerning approach to consuming digital content. It involves being actively selective about the sources of our information, seeking out those that are credible and trustworthy. This selectivity is not about limiting our exposure to different ideas, but about ensuring that the information we consume is reliable and informative.

In the Stoic practice, wisdom is closely tied to the concept of phronesis, or practical wisdom. Applying phronesis to our digital consumption means not just understanding information for its own sake but discerning its relevance and application in our lives. It involves asking ourselves how the information we consume impacts our beliefs, decisions, and actions. Does it contribute to our understanding of the world? Does it align with our values and principles? Does it enhance our capacity to live a good life?

Moreover, Stoic wisdom in the digital realm also involves being aware of cognitive biases, particularly confirmation bias, which can skew our perception of information. This bias leads us to favor information that confirms our preexisting beliefs and ignore or discount evidence that contradicts them. Recognizing and challenging our biases is crucial in developing a well-rounded understanding of the world.

Stoic wisdom also calls for humility in our approach to information. It reminds us that no matter how much we know, there is always more to learn. It encourages us to remain open to new ideas and perspectives, even those that challenge our existing beliefs. This openness is not about accepting every piece of information uncritically but about acknowledging the limits of our knowledge and being willing to expand it.

In summary, navigating the information landscape in the digital age with Stoic wisdom involves a combination of critical thinking, selective engagement, awareness of biases, and intellectual humility. It is about curating our digital consumption in a way that enriches our lives, broadens our understanding, and deepens our appreciation of the world and our place in it.

Responding to Misinformation

In the digital era, one of the significant challenges we face is the prevalence of misinformation. The ease with which content can be created and shared online has led to a proliferation of inaccurate, misleading, or even deliberately false information. As Stoics striving for wisdom, our response to this challenge is crucial, not only for our well-being but for the health of the broader digital community.

The Stoic approach to misinformation starts with the recognition of our responsibility in the information ecosystem. We are not just passive consumers of information but active participants in its dissemination. Therefore, it behooves us to practice due diligence before sharing or endorsing any content. This involves verifying the credibility of the source, cross-checking facts, and being cautious of content that triggers strong emotional reactions, as these are often used to manipulate or mislead.

When encountering misinformation, the Stoic practice of wisdom calls for a measured response. Instead of reacting impulsively with frustration or indignation, we should aim to respond with reason and clarity. This might involve providing correct information, pointing out inaccuracies, or simply choosing not to engage further when the discussion becomes unproductive.

However, responding to misinformation is not just about correcting falsehoods. It is also about understanding why people may believe and spread such information. Often, misinformation is rooted in deeper fears, uncertainties, or biases. Approaching these conversations with empathy and an attempt to understand the underlying concerns can be more effective than simply presenting facts.

Stoicism teaches us the importance of focusing on what is within our control. While we cannot control the spread of misinformation entirely, we can control our reactions to it and our actions in countering it. By responding to misinformation with wisdom, care, and responsibility, we contribute to a more informed and rational digital environment.

Moreover, engaging in the fight against misinformation aligns with the Stoic principle of contributing to the common good. By ensuring the accuracy and integrity of the information we share, we are not only practicing personal virtue but also serving the community. Our actions, no matter how small, can have a ripple effect in promoting a culture of truth and reason in the digital world.

Wisdom in Digital Communication

Applying Stoic wisdom in our digital communications involves more than just being selective and critical about the information we consume; it also encompasses how we express ourselves and interact with others online. In the Stoic philosophy, wisdom is not only about knowledge but also about acting and communicating in ways that reflect our rational and moral nature.

In the realm of digital communication, this means practicing thoughtfulness and intentionality in our interactions. Before posting, commenting, or responding online, we should pause and consider the impact of our words. Are they constructive? Do they contribute to a meaningful conversation? Are they aligned with our values and the person we aspire to be? Stoic wisdom teaches us to communicate not just for the sake of expression but for the purpose of positive and rational discourse.

This thoughtful approach to digital communication also involves being open to different viewpoints and engaging in dialogues that broaden our understanding. It means resisting the urge to engage in heated debates or arguments that lead nowhere but instead seeking discussions that are enlightening and enriching. The Stoic ideal of wisdom in communication is not about winning an argument or proving others wrong, but about learning, growing, and contributing to mutual understanding.

Wisdom in digital communication also calls for honesty and authenticity. In a space where it is easy to curate or conceal aspects of our lives, Stoic wisdom encourages us to present ourselves truthfully and authentically. This authenticity should not be mistaken for blunt or unfiltered expression. Instead, it's about being true to our values and expressing ourselves in ways that are respectful and considerate of others.

Lastly, Stoic wisdom in digital communication is about maintaining a sense of detachment and equanimity, especially in the face of conflict or criticism. Stoicism teaches us that while we can control our actions and words, we cannot control how others perceive or react to them. Therefore, we should communicate with the understanding that different perspectives and disagreements are natural, and our peace of mind should not be contingent on others' approval or agreement.

In summary, bringing wisdom to our digital communication is about creating a balance between honest self-expression and thoughtful consideration of others. It's about using our words to build rather than destroy, to educate rather than belittle, and to connect rather than alienate. Through this, we not only uphold the Stoic virtue of wisdom but also contribute to a more rational, respectful, and enriching digital world.

Understanding Digital Anxieties

In the digital age, a unique set of anxieties and pressures confront us, challenging our mental and emotional resilience. The Stoic virtue of courage becomes crucial in navigating these challenges. In Stoicism, courage is not just about bravery in the face of physical danger, but also about enduring and overcoming inner fears and anxieties, especially those arising from our digital engagements.

Digital anxieties can manifest in various forms: the fear of missing out (FOMO), anxiety over social media interactions, worries about online privacy, or stress from constant connectivity. These anxieties stem from the nature of digital platforms, which are designed to capture and retain our attention, often leading to an overinvestment in our online presence and interactions.

The Stoic approach to facing these digital anxieties involves first acknowledging and understanding them. It is about recognizing the sources of our digital stressors and confronting them with rationality and self-awareness. This process requires us to reflect on our digital habits and their impact on our well-being: Are we spending too much time online? Are our digital interactions meaningful or superficial? Are we letting online opinions and comparisons dictate our self-worth?

Stoicism teaches us to focus on what is within our control and to let go of what is not. In the context of digital anxieties, this means understanding that we cannot control the vast array of online content, the behavior of others on digital platforms, or the ever-changing trends and norms of the digital world. However, we can control our reactions to these stimuli, our engagement with digital platforms, and the boundaries we set for our digital consumption.

By applying the Stoic virtue of courage, we can confront our digital anxieties, not by avoiding or suppressing them, but by facing them with clarity and rationality. This approach allows us to use digital platforms in a way that benefits us, without letting them dominate our lives or disturb our peace of mind. Courage in the digital age is about finding the strength to maintain our authenticity, values, and tranquility in the face of the ever-evolving digital landscape.

Courage in Online Expression and Engagement

Exercising courage in the digital world extends beyond confronting anxieties; it also involves the bravery to express ourselves authentically and engage with others online in a meaningful way. In Stoicism, courage is not recklessness or fearlessness but the measured strength to act in accordance with one's principles, even in the face of opposition or criticism.

In the realm of social media and online platforms, expressing oneself authentically can be daunting. The fear of judgment, criticism, or backlash can lead to self-censorship or the portrayal of a curated persona that aligns with perceived social norms. Stoic courage in this context is about being true to oneself, sharing thoughts, opinions, and experiences honestly, while being mindful of how they contribute to the larger conversation.

This courage also involves standing up for what is right in the digital space. It might mean challenging misinformation, standing against online bullying, or supporting causes and movements that align with our values. This is not about engaging in every online battle but choosing our engagements wisely, with the intent to promote truth, understanding, and positive change.

Facing negative feedback or criticism is another aspect where courage is essential. In the digital world, feedback can be immediate and harsh, often amplified by the anonymity and distance that online platforms provide. A Stoic approach to handling criticism involves separating constructive feedback from mere trolling or unfounded criticism. It's about learning from valid points and letting go of negativity that serves no purpose other than to harm.

Additionally, Stoic courage in digital engagement is about the bravery to step back when necessary. In a world that often equates online presence with relevance or success, choosing to disconnect or reduce our digital footprint requires courage. It's a recognition that our worth is not determined by our online visibility but by living a life true to our principles and values.

In essence, courage in our digital expressions and engagements is about upholding our authenticity, defending what we believe in, and maintaining our integrity in the face of the unique challenges posed by the digital world. It's about using our digital platforms not just as a means of expression but as tools for positive influence and growth, both for ourselves and the broader digital community.

The Courage to Disconnect

In a world where digital connectivity is ever-present, one of the most courageous acts can be the decision to disconnect. The Stoic virtue of courage in this context is not just about facing fears or standing up for beliefs; it's also about recognizing when stepping away from digital platforms is necessary for our well-being and peace of mind. This form of courage challenges the modern narrative that equates constant online presence with productivity and success.

The Stoic principle of courage in disconnecting lies in acknowledging the value of solitude and reflection, away from the constant noise of the digital world. It's about understanding that our worth is not tied to how active we are online or how many notifications we receive. Disconnecting gives us the space to reconnect with ourselves, to engage in deep thinking, and to participate in activities that nourish our souls and bodies.

Moreover, the courage to disconnect involves overcoming the fear of missing out (FOMO). In a culture that constantly bombards us with updates and information, choosing to take a step back requires the strength to accept that we cannot be a part of everything. It's about finding contentment in the present moment and our immediate surroundings, rather than feeling compelled to be continuously connected to the digital world.

This act of disconnecting also allows us to cultivate real-world relationships and experiences. While digital platforms can provide a sense of connection, they often lack the depth and richness of face-to-face interactions. Courageously stepping away from screens enables us to engage more fully with the people and environment around us, fostering more meaningful and fulfilling experiences.

Additionally, disconnecting from digital devices and platforms can also be an act of self-care. In a world where online engagement can often lead to stress, anxiety, and information overload, taking regular breaks is essential for mental and emotional health. It's a recognition that to function at our best, we need to take care of our holistic well-being, which includes giving ourselves permission to unplug and recharge.

In essence, the courage to disconnect in the digital age is about asserting control over our digital lives. It's about making intentional choices regarding how, when, and why we engage with digital technology, ensuring that our use aligns with our values and contributes to our overall well-being. This courageous act is not about rejecting technology but about creating a balanced and healthy relationship with it.

Maintaining Personal Integrity Online

In the digital realm, where our actions and words can be amplified and preserved indefinitely, maintaining personal integrity becomes a paramount challenge. Stoic courage in this aspect is about upholding our values and principles, even when faced with the pressures and temptations of the online world. It is the steadfast commitment to being authentic and principled, regardless of the prevailing trends or norms on digital platforms.

Personal integrity online starts with self-awareness. It involves understanding our core values and principles and reflecting on how these should guide our digital interactions. This means being consistent in our actions and words, whether in private messages or public posts. It's about ensuring that our online persona aligns with who we are in the real world, resisting the urge to present a façade or alter our identity for wider acceptance or approval.

Stoic courage in maintaining integrity also involves the strength to resist peer pressure and the allure of following online trends that conflict with our values. In an environment where popularity and virality can be enticing, it takes courage to not compromise our principles for the sake of likes, shares, or followers. It's about recognizing that true self-worth comes from living in accordance with our virtues, not from external validation.

Furthermore, this integrity extends to how we treat others online. It means engaging with respect and kindness, avoiding the anonymity of the internet as an excuse for behavior that we wouldn't exhibit in person. It involves being honest in our communications and interactions, being accountable for our words and actions, and respecting the privacy and dignity of others.

The Stoic virtue of courage in maintaining personal integrity online also means having the bravery to admit mistakes and learn from them. In the fast-paced and often unforgiving world of social media, admitting faults can be difficult. However, acknowledging and learning from our errors is a critical aspect of personal growth and integrity.

In summary, maintaining personal integrity online is about embodying the Stoic virtues in our digital interactions. It's about being authentic, upholding our values, treating others with respect, and being accountable for our actions. This approach not only ensures that we act ethically and responsibly in the digital world but also contributes to a more trustworthy and respectful online community.

The Concept of Justice in Digital Spaces

In Stoic philosophy, justice is not only about legal or moral righteousness but encompasses a broader understanding of ethical behavior, fairness, and the betterment of society. In the context of digital spaces, practicing justice involves treating others with respect and empathy, fostering fairness and equality, and contributing to the overall health and positivity of online communities.

Digital justice starts with recognizing the inherent dignity and worth of every individual we interact with online. It means engaging with others respectfully, regardless of the anonymity and distance that digital platforms may provide. This respect extends to honoring differing opinions and perspectives, engaging in constructive dialogue rather than resorting to personal attacks or derogatory language.

Justice in digital interactions also involves being mindful of the content we share and the conversations we participate in. It's about ensuring that our digital footprint contributes to the well-being of others and the community as a whole. Practicing digital justice means standing against online harassment, bullying, and discrimination, and supporting those who are victims of such behaviors.

Furthermore, digital justice encompasses advocating for fairness and equality in online spaces. This includes challenging systemic issues such as the digital divide, which creates disparities in access to technology, or addressing biases in algorithms that can lead to unfair or prejudicial outcomes. It involves using our online presence to promote inclusivity, accessibility, and equitable treatment for all.

Practicing justice in the digital world also requires us to be conscious of the broader implications of our digital activities. This includes considering the environmental impact of our technology use, being aware of the ethical practices of the companies behind the platforms and devices we use, and understanding the global effects of our digital consumption.

In essence, practicing Stoic justice in digital spaces is about contributing to a more ethical, respectful, and equitable online world. It's about using our digital interactions to promote harmony, understanding, and the common good, upholding the Stoic ideal of living not just for ourselves but as part of a larger, interconnected community.

Ethical Behavior in the Digital Realm

Ethical behavior in digital interactions is a critical aspect of practicing Stoic justice. In the vast and complex realm of the internet, where our actions can have far-reaching consequences, behaving ethically is essential for maintaining the harmony and well-being of the online community.

One of the fundamental aspects of ethical digital behavior is honesty. This means being truthful in our communications and representations online. It involves avoiding deceitful practices, such as spreading false information, engaging in impersonation, or misrepresenting facts. Honesty in digital spaces builds trust and credibility, fostering a culture of integrity and reliability.

Respecting the privacy and consent of others is another crucial element of ethical behavior online. In a world where sharing information is just a click away, it's important to be mindful of what we share about others and how we use the information shared with us. This includes seeking permission before posting pictures or personal information about others and respecting their choices about digital privacy.

Ethical behavior also involves being aware of and adhering to the norms and guidelines of different digital platforms. This includes understanding and respecting the community standards of various social media sites, forums, and online groups. It's about contributing to these spaces in ways that are constructive, respectful, and in line with their intended purpose.

In addition, ethical digital behavior requires us to be conscious of the potential impact of our actions. This means considering how our words and actions might affect others, avoiding cyberbullying, harassment, or any form of online abuse. It's about using digital platforms to uplift and support, rather than to harm or degrade.

Lastly, ethical behavior in the digital world involves advocating for and upholding principles of fairness and justice. This can include standing against unjust practices online, such as censorship, unjust surveillance, or the spread of hate speech. It's about using our digital presence to promote a more just, respectful, and ethical online environment.

In summary, ethical behavior in the digital realm, as guided by Stoic justice, is about being truthful, respectful, mindful, and fair in our digital interactions. It's about aligning our online conduct with our principles and contributing positively to the digital communities we are part of. Through ethical behavior, we uphold the Stoic ideal of justice, fostering a digital world that is equitable, trustworthy, and harmonious.

Promoting Equality and Inclusivity Online

In the pursuit of Stoic justice in the digital realm, promoting equality and inclusivity is paramount. The internet, as a global platform, has the potential to be a space of unparalleled diversity and representation. However, this potential can only be realized when we actively work to make digital spaces more inclusive and equitable for all.

Promoting equality online starts with recognizing and challenging the biases that exist in digital communities and algorithms. These biases, whether based on race, gender, sexuality, religion, or other factors, can lead to unequal representation and discrimination. A Stoic approach to justice involves being aware of these biases and advocating for changes that ensure fair and equitable treatment for all users.

Inclusivity in digital spaces also means creating and supporting environments where diverse voices and perspectives are heard and valued. This involves not only listening to and amplifying marginalized voices but also challenging practices and behaviors that silence or exclude them. It's about fostering online communities where everyone feels welcome and safe to express themselves.

Another aspect of promoting digital equality and inclusivity is ensuring accessibility. This means advocating for and implementing design and content choices that make digital platforms accessible to all, including people with disabilities. From website design to social media posts, ensuring that digital content is accessible to everyone is a crucial part of creating an inclusive online environment.

Inclusivity also involves being mindful of the global nature of the internet. It requires an understanding and respect for cultural differences and an awareness that digital content and communication may be interpreted differently across cultures. This global perspective encourages us to engage with others online in a way that is respectful of these differences and fosters mutual understanding.

By promoting equality and inclusivity in digital spaces, we uphold the Stoic virtue of justice, contributing to a digital world that is fairer and more representative of the diverse tapestry of human society. It's about using our online presence and actions to create a more inclusive and equitable digital environment for everyone.

The Need for Moderation in Digital Use

In the Stoic practice, temperance, or moderation, is a key virtue. In the digital world, this virtue becomes essential in managing our engagement with technology. The need for moderation in digital use stems from the recognition that while technology offers numerous benefits, excessive or unbalanced use can lead to negative consequences for our mental, emotional, and even physical well-being.

The concept of moderation in digital use is not about completely shunning technology; rather, it's about finding a healthy balance. It involves being mindful of the amount of time we spend online and the nature of our digital activities. Are we using technology in a way that enriches our lives and aligns with our goals, or are we mindlessly scrolling through feeds, leading to wasted time and a sense of dissatisfaction?

Moderation also means being aware of the impact of digital technology on our mental health. Excessive use of digital devices, especially before bedtime, can disrupt sleep patterns and lead to sleep deprivation. Constant connectivity can create a sense of being always 'on,' leading to stress and burnout. By practicing moderation, we can mitigate these risks, ensuring that our technology use is sustainable and healthful.

Practicing digital temperance also involves creating boundaries around our use of technology. This could mean setting specific times for checking emails and social media, taking regular breaks from screens, or designating tech-free zones and times, such as during meals or family time. These boundaries help to prevent digital technology from encroaching on every aspect of our lives, allowing us to be present in the moment and engage more fully with the world around us.

In addition to these personal practices, moderation in digital use also extends to how we consume content. It's about choosing quality over quantity, engaging with content that is informative, inspiring, or entertaining, rather than passively consuming whatever is put in front of us. This selective engagement not only makes our digital time more fulfilling but also helps in avoiding information overload and the stress that comes with it.

In essence, the need for moderation in digital use is about applying the Stoic virtue of temperance to our technology habits. It's about using technology intentionally and mindfully, ensuring that it serves us, rather than us becoming servants to it. By practicing digital temperance, we can enjoy the benefits of technology while maintaining our health, well-being, and peace of mind.

Practical Tips for Digital Moderation

Implementing the Stoic virtue of temperance in our digital lives requires practical strategies. These strategies are not about drastic measures but about making small, sustainable changes that can lead to a more balanced digital life. Here are some practical tips to help moderate digital consumption:

Set Time Limits: Use built-in smartphone or application features to set daily limits for app usage. Once the limit is reached, make a conscious effort to disengage from the device. This helps in controlling the amount of time spent on digital platforms and encourages more mindful use of technology.

Designate Tech-Free Times: Establish certain times of the day as tech-free. This could be during meals, the first hour after waking up, or before bedtime. These tech-free moments allow for disconnection from the digital world and reconnection with the immediate physical environment.

Mindful Notifications: Adjust notification settings to receive only essential alerts. Constant notifications can create a sense of urgency and distract from important tasks or moments. By controlling what alerts you receive, you can reduce distractions and improve focus.

Digital Detoxes: Periodically engage in digital detoxes. This could be a day each week or a few hours each day where you consciously stay away from digital devices. These detox periods provide a break from digital stimuli and offer space for other activities.

Quality Content Consumption: Be selective about the content you consume. Prioritize content that is enriching, educational, or truly enjoyable. Avoid aimless browsing or consuming content that doesn't add value to your life.

Physical Activity: Incorporate physical activity into your routine. Regular exercise, whether it's a walk, yoga, or a workout session, can serve as a healthy break from screen time and boost overall well-being.

Engage in Non-Digital Hobbies: Invest time in hobbies or activities that don't involve screens. Reading, painting, cooking, or gardening can offer a refreshing change and reduce reliance on digital entertainment.

Social Media Curating: Curate your social media feeds to follow accounts that inspire, educate, or uplift you. Unfollow or mute accounts that trigger negative emotions or are not beneficial to your well-being.

Mindful Browsing: Practice intentional browsing. Before opening a browser or an app, take a moment to think about what you're looking for or why you're engaging with the device.

Sleep Hygiene: Avoid screens at least an hour before bedtime to improve sleep quality. Consider reading a book or practicing relaxation techniques instead of using a digital device.

By incorporating these tips into your daily life, you can practice the Stoic virtue of temperance in the digital realm. It's about making intentional choices regarding digital use, leading to a more balanced, productive, and fulfilling digital life.

Mindful Engagement with Technology

Mindful engagement with technology is a key aspect of practicing digital temperance. It involves being present and intentional with our use of digital devices, ensuring that our interactions with technology are purposeful and aligned with our values and goals. This mindful approach helps to prevent mindless scrolling and excessive use, fostering a healthier relationship with our digital tools.

To cultivate mindful engagement, start by reflecting on the purpose of each digital interaction. Before opening an app or browsing a website, consider what you hope to achieve. Are you looking for information, connecting with friends, or just filling time? Being clear about your intentions can help guide a more meaningful and controlled use of technology.

Another aspect of mindful engagement is being aware of our emotional and mental states while using digital devices. Notice if certain apps or websites trigger negative feelings such as anxiety, envy, or anger. Being conscious of these emotional responses allows us to make more informed decisions about which platforms are beneficial for us and which ones we might need to limit or avoid.

Practicing mindfulness also involves being aware of our physical presence while engaging with technology. Pay attention to your posture, your breathing, and any signs of physical discomfort. This awareness can help prevent the physical strain associated with prolonged use of digital devices, such as eye strain, neck pain, or wrist discomfort.

Incorporating mindfulness techniques, such as meditation or deep breathing, can enhance our ability to engage with technology mindfully. Taking short breaks to practice these techniques can help reset our focus and reduce the stress that can come with continuous digital consumption.

Finally, mindful engagement with technology means knowing when to disconnect. It's recognizing when digital interactions are no longer serving a positive purpose and having the discipline to step away. This could mean setting specific times for digital use or creating tech-free zones in our daily routine.

By embracing a mindful approach to our digital interactions, we are not only practicing the Stoic virtue of temperance but also enhancing our overall digital experience. Mindful engagement allows us to use technology as a tool that benefits and enriches our lives, rather than as a source of distraction or stress.

Cultivating a Balanced Digital Lifestyle

The final step in applying Stoic temperance to our digital lives is cultivating a balanced digital lifestyle. This balance is about integrating technology into our lives in a way that enhances rather than detracts from our overall well-being. It involves creating a harmony between our digital interactions and our physical, emotional, and spiritual health.

Creating a balanced digital lifestyle starts with setting priorities. Determine what is truly important in your life and how digital tools can support these priorities. Technology should be a means to enrich your life, not an end in itself. Whether it's using digital tools for learning, staying connected with loved ones, or managing your work efficiently, ensure that your digital habits align with your life's goals and values.

Next, create a routine that incorporates both digital and non-digital activities. Balance your day with periods of focused work, leisure, physical activity, and rest. Use technology to enhance these activities, but don't let it dominate your time. Regularly assess your routine and adjust as necessary to maintain a healthy balance.

Also, consider the quality of your digital interactions. Engage in online activities that are fulfilling and leave you feeling positive. Avoid digital content that drains your energy or provokes negativity. Remember, not all screen time is created equal; choose quality over quantity.

Maintaining social connections outside of the digital realm is also vital. While technology can help us stay connected with distant friends and family, it cannot fully replace the depth and richness of face-to-face interactions. Make time for in-person connections, as these are crucial for emotional and social well-being.

Finally, embrace the concept of digital minimalism. This doesn't mean eliminating technology but rather simplifying your digital life to include only what truly adds value. Regularly review your digital tools and platforms, keeping only those that serve a purpose and discarding the rest.

In summary, cultivating a balanced digital lifestyle is about finding the right mix of online and offline activities that support your overall well-being. It's about using technology mindfully and intentionally, ensuring that it serves as a tool for a fulfilling and virtuous life. Through this balanced approach, we can embrace the benefits of the digital age without losing sight of the Stoic principles that guide us towards a meaningful existence.

Chapter 4: Practical Applications

The journey into Stoicism is not just a theoretical exploration but a practical endeavor. Daily Stoic practices are the cornerstone of integrating this ancient philosophy into our modern lives. These practices are not about grand gestures or profound transformations overnight; rather, they are about small, consistent acts that gradually align our thoughts and actions with Stoic principles.

Incorporating Stoic exercises into our daily routine helps us cultivate virtues like wisdom, courage, temperance, and justice. These virtues, when practiced regularly, become more than abstract concepts; they transform into tangible guides that steer our actions and reactions, especially in the context of the challenges posed by the digital age.

The essence of daily Stoic practice lies in its simplicity and applicability. Whether it's a morning meditation reflecting on what's within our control, an evening review of our actions and their alignment with our principles, or mindful pauses throughout the day to reconnect with our intentions, each practice serves as a step towards a more stoic and balanced life.

As we embark on these daily exercises, it's important to approach them with patience and kindness towards ourselves. Change, especially at the fundamental level of beliefs and behaviors, takes time. The aim is not to attain perfection but to make gradual progress, consistently aligning our actions with our ideals.

In the following pages, we will explore various daily exercises that embody the essence of Stoicism. These practices will serve as tools to cultivate a stoic mindset, helping us navigate the complexities and challenges of life in the digital age with equanimity, clarity, and purpose.

Mindfulness and Awareness Exercises

At the heart of Stoicism is the practice of mindfulness and self-awareness, essential for understanding our reactions and controlling them. By cultivating mindfulness, we learn to live in the present moment, observing our thoughts, feelings, and actions without immediate judgment or reaction. This heightened state of awareness is pivotal in practicing Stoicism, especially in the context of the digital world, where distractions are frequent and overwhelming.

Mindfulness Meditation: Begin by setting aside a few minutes each day for mindfulness meditation. This practice involves focusing on your breath and observing your thoughts as they arise, without getting attached to them. It helps in developing a sense of calm and presence, essential for dealing with digital distractions and information overload.

Stoic Reflection: At the end of each day, engage in a Stoic reflection. Review the day's events, your reactions to them, and how they aligned with your Stoic principles. This exercise not only promotes self-awareness but also helps in recognizing patterns in behavior and thought that you may wish to change.

Mindful Breathing: Throughout the day, especially during moments of stress or high emotion, practice mindful breathing. Take a moment to focus solely on your breath, inhaling and exhaling slowly. This simple practice can be a powerful tool in regaining your composure and refocusing your mind.

Presence in the Moment: Consciously practice being present in your daily activities. Whether it's during a conversation, a meal, or a walk, fully engage with the experience, free from digital distractions. This practice of presence enriches your experiences and helps combat the continuous partial attention common in digital interactions.

Body Scan Meditation: Incorporate a body scan meditation into your routine. This involves paying attention to different parts of your body, noticing any sensations or tensions. It's a practice that fosters a deeper connection between mind and body and can be particularly helpful in alleviating the physical strains of prolonged digital device usage.

By incorporating these mindfulness and awareness exercises into your daily routine, you cultivate a key aspect of Stoicism. These practices enhance your ability to remain present, aware, and in control of your reactions, providing a foundation for living a Stoic life in the digital age. They offer a means to navigate the constant flow of information and interaction with a clear, focused, and balanced mind.

Exercises for Developing Self-Control and Discipline

Self-control and discipline are fundamental Stoic virtues, particularly vital in navigating the digital age. The online world, with its endless temptations and distractions, requires us to exercise a high degree of self-control to remain focused and aligned with our values. Here are some exercises to strengthen these essential qualities:

Voluntary Discomfort: Practice the Stoic exercise of voluntary discomfort to enhance self-discipline. This could involve limiting your use of certain digital devices or intentionally abstaining from social media for a set period. The purpose is not to create hardship for its own sake but to remind yourself that you can exercise control over your desires and impulses.

Setting Digital Boundaries: Establish clear boundaries for your digital consumption. This might involve designated times for checking emails or social media, or not using digital devices during meals or right before bed. Adhering to these self-imposed rules strengthens your discipline and helps prevent digital overindulgence.

Delayed Gratification: Implement practices of delayed gratification in your daily life. For example, before indulging in a session of browsing or gaming, complete a task or a chore that you have been postponing. This practice not only helps in getting things done but also reinforces the ability to control impulses and prioritize long-term benefits over immediate pleasures.

Focused Task Completion: Develop the habit of completing tasks without succumbing to digital distractions. When working on a task, commit to focused work for a set period without checking your phone or browsing the internet. Gradually increase this duration to build your capacity for sustained concentration.

Mindful Consumption: Be mindful of the content you consume online. Instead of aimlessly scrolling through feeds, choose to engage with content that is educational, uplifting, or aligns with your interests. This conscious choice in consumption fosters self-control in resisting the lure of less meaningful content.

Through these exercises, you cultivate the Stoic virtues of self-control and discipline, essential for maintaining focus and purpose in a world filled with digital distractions. By regularly practicing these exercises, you reinforce your ability to make choices that are in line with your values and goals, leading to a more balanced and fulfilling digital life.

Gratitude and Positive Reflection

Incorporating gratitude and positive reflection into daily life is a powerful Stoic practice, particularly effective in counteracting the negativity bias often exacerbated by digital interactions. By focusing on the positive aspects and cultivating a sense of gratitude, we can maintain a balanced perspective and enhance our overall well-being.

Daily Gratitude Exercise: Start or end your day by listing three things you are grateful for. These can be as simple as a sunny day, a productive work session, or a meaningful conversation. This practice shifts focus from what's lacking or problematic to what's abundant and positive in your life.

Reflecting on Positive Interactions: Make it a habit to reflect on positive digital interactions each day. Whether it's a supportive comment, an informative article, or a funny video, acknowledging these positive experiences can help mitigate the impact of negative online content.

Journaling Positive Experiences: Keep a journal where you record positive experiences, thoughts, and feelings. This can include accomplishments, moments of happiness, or instances of personal growth. Reviewing this journal can provide a boost during challenging times and remind you of the positive aspects of your life.

Recognizing Growth and Learning: Regularly acknowledge your growth and learning, especially in the context of digital challenges. Whether it's successfully managing a digital detox, overcoming a piece of misinformation, or engaging in a constructive online debate, recognizing these victories fosters a sense of accomplishment and progress.

Sharing Gratitude with Others: Express gratitude towards others, both in the digital and physical worlds. This could be thanking someone for their helpful advice online or showing appreciation for a colleague's assistance. Expressing gratitude not only uplifts others but also reinforces your own feelings of thankfulness.

Through these practices of gratitude and positive reflection, you can cultivate a more optimistic and appreciative mindset. This approach not only aligns with Stoic principles but also serves as an antidote to the negativity that can pervade our digital lives. By regularly focusing on the positive, you build a foundation of resilience and contentment, essential for navigating the complexities of the modern world.

Empathy and Understanding Others

Developing empathy and understanding is a key aspect of Stoicism, particularly relevant in our digital interactions. In a realm where people are often reduced to usernames or profiles, practicing empathy is essential for meaningful and compassionate online engagement. Here are some exercises to cultivate this important virtue:

Active Listening in Digital Conversations: Practice active listening during online interactions. This means fully engaging with the other person's message, seeking to understand their perspective before responding. It's easy to misinterpret or skim through messages in digital communication; taking the time to truly understand can lead to more empathetic and meaningful exchanges.

Perspective-Taking: When encountering differing opinions online, take a moment to consider the other person's viewpoint. Ask yourself why they might hold that perspective and what experiences or information led them to it. This practice doesn't mean you have to agree, but it fosters a deeper understanding and empathy for others.

Reflecting on Shared Humanity: Regularly remind yourself of the shared humanity behind each digital profile. Recognize that each person you interact with has their own struggles, joys, and complexities. This recognition can help cultivate empathy and patience in digital interactions.

Mindful Response Practice: Before responding to comments or messages, especially in heated discussions, take a moment to pause and reflect. Consider how your words might affect the other person, and choose responses that are empathetic and constructive.

Engaging in Diverse Communities: Broaden your digital horizons by engaging with online communities different from your usual circles. This exposure to diverse perspectives and experiences can enhance your understanding and empathy for people from different backgrounds.

By practicing empathy and striving to understand others in our digital interactions, we not only uphold Stoic principles but also contribute to a more compassionate and respectful online environment. Empathy allows us to connect with others on a deeper level, fostering a sense of community and shared understanding in an increasingly digital world.

Dealing with Information Overload

In the digital age, one of the most common challenges is managing the overwhelming flow of information, often referred to as information overload. Stoicism, with its emphasis on rationality and focus, offers valuable strategies to navigate this inundation of data. These Stoic strategies can help us process information effectively without becoming overwhelmed or stressed.

Selective Engagement: Practice selective engagement with information. Not all data and news require your attention or reaction. Identify what information is relevant to your life, work, and well-being, and focus primarily on these sources.

Setting Information Boundaries: Establish clear boundaries for news and social media consumption. Allocate specific times for checking news or browsing social media. Avoid starting or ending your day with news consumption, as it can lead to increased stress.

Quality over Quantity: Choose quality sources of information over a sheer quantity of data. Subscribe to news sources that are known for their credibility and thorough reporting. Limit the number of sources to avoid redundancy and focus on those that offer valuable insights.

Mindful Consumption: Be mindful of how information affects you emotionally and mentally. If certain topics consistently lead to stress or anxiety, it's okay to take a break from them. Protecting your mental well-being is more important than staying constantly updated.

Reflection and Analysis: Regularly take time to reflect on the information you consume. Think critically about the news and articles you read. Question the source, the intent, and the implications of the information. This reflective practice encourages deeper understanding and prevents passive consumption.

Applying these Stoic strategies to manage information overload can lead to a more balanced and thoughtful approach to news and data consumption. By controlling the flow of information and focusing on what truly matters, you can maintain clarity of mind and make more informed decisions in both your digital and offline life.

Navigating Social Media Mindfully

Social media is a dominant aspect of the digital age, offering both opportunities for connection and challenges in maintaining our well-being. A Stoic approach to social media involves navigating these platforms mindfully, ensuring that our engagement is intentional and aligns with our values. Here are some strategies for mindful social media use:

Intentional Usage: Before logging into social media, set a clear intention for your use. Are you logging in to check on a friend, to gather news, or for entertainment? Understanding your purpose can help guide a more focused and meaningful use of social media.

Time Management: Allocate specific times for social media use and stick to them. Avoid endless scrolling by setting time limits for each session. This practice not only helps in managing time effectively but also prevents social media from encroaching on other important aspects of life.

Content Curation: Actively curate your social media feed. Follow accounts that inspire, educate, and uplift you. Unfollow or mute accounts that consistently provoke negative emotions or do not align with your interests or values.

Engagement Choices: Be selective in your interactions on social media. Engage in discussions that are constructive and align with your interests and values. Avoid getting drawn into arguments or negative exchanges that lead nowhere and only serve to increase stress.

Gratitude and Positivity: Use social media as a platform for spreading positivity and gratitude. Share content that is uplifting, express appreciation for others, and contribute to a positive online environment.

Reflection Post-Use: After using social media, take a moment to reflect on the experience. Did it align with your intention? How do you feel emotionally? This reflection can provide insights into your social media habits and guide future use.

By applying these Stoic practices to social media use, you can navigate these platforms more mindfully. This approach helps in maintaining a healthy balance, ensuring that social media is a tool for positive connection and growth, rather than a source of stress or negativity.

Handling Online Negativity and Conflict

In the realm of digital communication, encountering negativity and conflict is almost inevitable. The anonymity and distance provided by screens can sometimes lead to harsher interactions than we might experience in person. Stoicism, with its emphasis on rationality and inner peace, offers valuable guidance on how to handle such online negativity and conflict.

Rational Response Over Emotional Reaction: When faced with negative comments or online conflict, take a moment to pause before responding. Stoicism teaches us to respond with reason rather than reacting emotionally. Consider the intent behind the comment and whether a response would be constructive.

Reflecting on Control: Remember the Stoic principle of focusing on what you can control. You cannot control others' opinions or behavior online, but you can control your reaction to them. Sometimes, the wisest action might be not to engage at all.

Seeking Constructive Outcomes: If you choose to respond to negativity or conflict, aim for a resolution or constructive outcome. Approach the conversation with the intent to understand and clarify, not to win an argument or prove the other person wrong.

Empathy and Understanding: Try to understand the perspective of the other person. They might be acting out of their own frustrations or misunderstandings. Empathy can often defuse conflict and lead to more productive dialogues.

Setting Boundaries: It's important to set boundaries for acceptable behavior in your digital interactions. Do not tolerate abusive or harmful behavior. Know when to disengage from a conversation or block users if necessary for your mental well-being.

Reflecting Post-Interaction: After an encounter with negativity or conflict, take time to reflect. Consider what you learned from the interaction and how it aligns with your Stoic practice. This reflection can be a valuable tool for personal growth and resilience.

Handling online negativity and conflict with a Stoic approach allows you to maintain your composure and integrity. It enables you to navigate the digital world with a sense of calm and rationality, preserving your inner peace amidst external turmoil.

Managing Digital Distractions and Procrastination

In the age of digital technology, distractions are a constant challenge, often leading to procrastination and reduced productivity. Stoicism, with its focus on discipline and living purposefully, offers strategies to manage these challenges effectively. Here are some Stoic-inspired techniques to overcome digital distractions and procrastination:

Creating a Structured Routine: Establish a daily routine that includes designated times for work and leisure. Having a clear structure helps prevent aimless browsing and falling into the trap of digital distractions.

Prioritizing Tasks: Start your day by identifying the most important tasks. Focus on completing these tasks before allowing yourself time on digital platforms. This prioritization ensures that your most significant work isn't overshadowed by less important but more immediately gratifying digital activities.

Single-Tasking: Practice single-tasking rather than multi-tasking. Focus on one task at a time, giving it your full attention. This approach is more effective and aligns with the Stoic principle of doing everything with purpose and attention.

Using Technology Mindfully: Utilize technology as a tool to aid productivity rather than a source of distraction. This might involve using apps that block distracting websites during work hours or turning off non-essential notifications.

Reflective Pauses: Regularly pause to reflect on your current activity. Ask yourself if this is the best use of your time and if it aligns with your goals. This practice of self-reflection helps maintain focus and prevents mindless digital engagement.

Rewarding Progress: Reward yourself for completing tasks or staying focused for a set period. These rewards can be small breaks or engaging in a preferred digital activity. This system of rewards can motivate you to stay on task and reduce procrastination.

By implementing these practices, you can better manage digital distractions and procrastination, aligning your daily actions with your larger goals and values. These strategies not only enhance productivity but also foster a sense of accomplishment and purpose in your digital engagements.

Balancing Digital Life with Real World Interactions

Finding a healthy balance between digital engagements and real-world interactions is crucial in the digital age. While technology offers incredible opportunities for connectivity and access to information, it's important not to let it overshadow the richness of face-to-face interactions and physical experiences. Here are some Stoic strategies to help maintain this balance:

Prioritizing In-Person Connections: Make a conscious effort to prioritize in-person interactions with family, friends, and colleagues. These real-world connections are vital for emotional well-being and can offer a depth of interaction that digital communication often lacks.

Engaging in Physical Activities: Regularly participate in physical activities, be it exercise, outdoor adventures, or simply taking walks. Physical activities not only provide a break from screens but also contribute to physical and mental health.

Practicing Mindful Technology Use: Be mindful of the role technology plays in your life. Use it purposefully, whether for work, learning, or staying connected with loved ones. Avoid letting it become a default activity that fills up all your free time.

Creating Tech-Free Zones: Establish tech-free zones or times in your home, such as during meals or family gatherings. These moments allow for undistracted engagement with those around you and foster a sense of presence and connection.

Balancing Online and Offline Hobbies: Cultivate hobbies that don't involve screens, such as reading, cooking, gardening, or playing a musical instrument. These activities offer a fulfilling and balancing counterpoint to the digital aspects of life.

Reflecting on Digital Consumption: Regularly reflect on your digital consumption and its impact on your life. Ask yourself if your current digital habits support your overall well-being and align with your values. Adjust as needed to ensure a healthy balance.

By consciously applying these Stoic practices, you can create a more harmonious balance between your digital life and real-world interactions. This balance is key to ensuring that technology enhances rather than detracts from the quality of your life, allowing you to live more fully in both the digital and physical realms.

The Role of Reflection in Stoicism

Reflection is a fundamental aspect of Stoic practice, essential for personal growth and the application of Stoic principles. Regular self-reflection helps us to gain insight into our behaviors, thoughts, and emotions, allowing us to live more intentionally and in alignment with our values. In the digital age, where we are constantly bombarded with information and stimuli, taking time to reflect becomes even more crucial.

Reflection in Stoicism is not just about introspection; it's a practical tool for self-improvement. By regularly examining our actions and attitudes, we can identify areas where we are not living according to Stoic principles and make necessary adjustments. This process of reflection helps us to become more mindful of our reactions to both online and offline experiences, enabling us to respond with reason and wisdom.

The practice of daily reflection can take many forms. It might involve reviewing the events of the day each evening, contemplating how we handled various situations, and considering ways we could have responded more in line with Stoic virtues. It could also involve reflecting on our digital habits, examining how our time spent online aligns with our overall goals and values.

Reflection also allows us to appreciate our progress. Recognizing and celebrating our successes in applying Stoic principles, no matter how small, can be motivating and reinforcing. It reminds us that personal growth is a continuous journey, one in which each step forward is significant.

Incorporating regular reflection into our daily routine is a powerful way to deepen our understanding and practice of Stoicism. It helps us to remain grounded and focused on our path to living a virtuous and meaningful life, amidst the distractions and challenges of the digital world.

Journaling Prompts for Self-Awareness

Journaling is an effective tool for enhancing self-awareness, a key component of Stoic practice. It provides a space for personal reflection and exploration, allowing us to gain deeper insights into our thoughts, behaviors, and reactions, especially in the context of our digital interactions. Here are some journaling prompts designed to foster self-awareness:

Digital Reflection: How does my time spent online align with my values and goals? Are there changes I can make to ensure a healthier digital lifestyle?

Control and Influence: What aspects of my digital interactions can I control, and which are beyond my influence? How can I focus more on what is within my control?

Emotional Responses: What emotions do I commonly experience during my digital interactions? Are these emotions reflective of how I want to feel?

Stoic Virtues: How did I practice the Stoic virtues of wisdom, courage, justice, and temperance in my digital interactions today? What could I have done differently?

Mindfulness: When am I most likely to use digital devices mindlessly? What strategies can I implement to be more mindful of my technology use?

Reactions to Challenges: How do I typically react to challenges or negativity encountered online? How could a Stoic perspective alter my response?

Gratitude: What aspects of technology am I grateful for? How has digital technology positively impacted my life?

Learning and Growth: What have I learned from my digital experiences? How have these experiences contributed to my personal growth?

Balance: How balanced is my digital life with my offline activities and relationships? What steps can I take to create a better balance?

Aspirations: How can I use digital platforms to support my personal and professional aspirations?

Using these prompts regularly can help cultivate a deeper self-awareness and understanding of how our digital lives intersect with our Stoic practice. Through reflective journaling, we can uncover insights that guide us in aligning our digital habits with our journey towards living a virtuous and fulfilling life.

Prompts for Exploring Emotions and Reactions

Understanding and managing our emotions is a fundamental aspect of Stoic practice. The digital world, with its unique challenges and stimuli, can often trigger a wide range of emotions. Journaling about these emotions and our reactions to digital experiences can provide valuable insights into our inner workings and help us cultivate a more Stoic approach to life. Here are some prompts to guide this exploration:

Identifying Triggers: What specific content or interactions online tend to trigger negative emotions in me? Why do I think these particular things affect me this way?

Emotional Patterns: Are there patterns in my emotional responses to digital content? How do these patterns reflect my underlying beliefs or values?

Reaction vs. Response: Can I recall a recent instance where I reacted emotionally to something online? How could I have responded differently with a Stoic perspective?

Managing Emotions: What strategies have I found effective in managing strong emotions that arise from digital interactions? How can I further develop these strategies?

Empathy in Digital Spaces: How do I feel when I encounter differing opinions or conflicts online? How can I practice empathy in these situations?

Learning from Emotions: What have my emotions taught me about my relationship with digital technology? How can I use this understanding to improve my digital well-being?

Stress and Relaxation: What digital activities cause me stress? Conversely, what online activities bring me relaxation or joy?

Transforming Reactions: How can I use Stoic principles to transform my emotional reactions into more rational and constructive responses?

Digital Detachment: How do I feel during periods of digital detachment or disconnection? What does this tell me about my relationship with technology?

Growth and Challenges: What challenges have I faced in the digital realm,

and how have they contributed to my
personal growth?

Reflecting on these prompts can help you develop
a deeper understanding of your emotions and
reactions within the digital context. By exploring
and analyzing these aspects of your experience,
you can cultivate a more Stoic approach to your
digital life, characterized by rationality, emotional
intelligence, and inner peace.

Reflecting on Relationships and Interactions

Stoicism emphasizes the importance of our
relationships and interactions with others,
advocating for treating people with respect,
empathy, and kindness. In the digital age, where
interactions can often become impersonal or
misinterpreted, reflecting on these aspects is
crucial. Journaling about our relationships and
interactions, both online and offline, can offer
insights into how we connect with others and how
we can improve these connections. Here are some
prompts to facilitate this reflection:

Quality of Interactions: How do my
online interactions compare in quality to my
in-person interactions? What differences do I

notice, and what might be the reason for these differences?

Impact of Digital Communication: How has digital communication affected my relationships with friends, family, and colleagues? Has it brought me closer to some people or created distance with others?

Empathy and Understanding: How well do I feel I understand and empathize with others in my digital communications? Are there times when I might have misinterpreted someone's words or intentions online?

Conflict Resolution: Reflect on a recent conflict or misunderstanding you had online. How did you handle it? Looking back, how could you have applied Stoic principles to resolve it more effectively?

Support and Community: How do I contribute to creating a supportive and positive environment in my online communities? Are there ways I can improve my contributions?

Balancing Relationships: How do I balance my time between online interactions and spending time with people in my physical surroundings? Are there changes I need to make to strike a better balance?

Influence of Social Media: How does social media affect my perception of others and myself? Do I find myself making comparisons, and how does this impact my relationships?

Communication Skills: What have I learned about my communication skills through my digital interactions? Are there areas where I could improve or strengths I can build upon?

Gratitude in Relationships: What relationships am I particularly grateful for, and why? How often do I express this gratitude, either online or in person?

Personal Growth in Interactions: How have my digital and in-person interactions contributed to my personal growth? What lessons have I learned from the people I interact with?

Reflecting on these aspects of your relationships and interactions can deepen your understanding of how you connect with others and how you can apply Stoic principles to enhance these connections. It can lead to more meaningful, empathetic, and fulfilling relationships, both in the digital world and beyond.

Contemplating Life Goals and Aspirations

Reflection on our life goals and aspirations is essential for ensuring that our daily actions, including our digital habits, align with our broader purposes and values. Stoicism teaches us to live intentionally and purposefully, focusing on what truly matters. Journaling about our goals and aspirations can provide clarity and motivation, helping us to navigate our lives with direction and meaning. Here are some prompts to guide this contemplative process:

Alignment of Actions: How do my daily activities, especially my digital habits, align with my long-term goals and aspirations? Are there discrepancies, and how can I address them?

Defining Success: How do I define success in my life, and how does this definition influence my online behavior and choices?

Personal Growth: In what ways do I wish to grow personally and professionally?

How can my digital interactions support this growth?

Life Priorities: What are my top priorities in life? How well do my digital engagements reflect these priorities?

Overcoming Obstacles: What obstacles or challenges am I currently facing in achieving my goals, and how can Stoic principles help me overcome them?

Vision of the Future: How do I envision my life in the next five to ten years? What role does technology play in this vision?

Learning and Development: What skills or knowledge do I wish to acquire, and how can I utilize digital resources to aid in this learning?

Contributions to Society: How do I wish to contribute to my community or society? Are there ways I can use digital platforms to make a positive impact?

Work-Life Balance: How do I maintain a healthy work-life balance, and what role does technology play in this balance?

Reflecting on Achievements: What are my most significant achievements to date, and how have my digital interactions contributed to these successes?

By contemplating these aspects of your life, you can ensure that your daily actions, including your digital engagements, are in harmony with your deeper goals and aspirations. This alignment is key to living a fulfilling and Stoic life, where every action is purposeful and every choice is a step towards your envisioned future.

Chapter 5: Case Studies

In today's digital age, one of the most common challenges is managing distractions, especially in a work-from-home environment. This story begins with Alex, a marketing professional, who found himself struggling with the blurred lines between personal and professional life while working from home. Constant notifications, social media, and the lure of the internet were a continuous source of distraction.

Alex's journey into Stoicism started with his search for strategies to enhance productivity and maintain a work-life balance. He stumbled upon the Stoic practice of discipline and focus, which resonated with his struggle. Alex began to implement these Stoic principles by setting clear boundaries for his work hours and personal time. He designated a specific area in his home as his workspace, symbolically separating it from his living space.

He also adopted the Stoic practice of premeditatio malorum, where he would start his day by anticipating potential distractions and planning ways to address them. This included turning off non-essential notifications during work hours and using website blockers to minimize the temptation of aimless browsing.

One of the key Stoic principles Alex embraced was the focus on what is within his control. He accepted that while he couldn't eliminate all distractions, he could control his response to them. This mindset shift was crucial in transforming his approach to work and productivity.

By integrating these Stoic practices into his daily routine, Alex found a significant improvement in his ability to focus and in his overall productivity. His story is a testament to how ancient Stoic wisdom can be applied effectively in the modern digital context to overcome challenges like digital distractions.

Managing Online Negativity: A Story of Cyberbullying

Emma, a high school teacher, faced the daunting challenge of cyberbullying. As someone who actively used social media for educational purposes and personal connections, she suddenly found herself the target of anonymous negative comments and harassing messages online. The experience was jarring, affecting her confidence and emotional well-being.

In her search for ways to cope, Emma discovered Stoicism, which offered a different perspective on handling adversity, including the kind faced online. Stoic teachings on resilience and emotional control became her tools in navigating this difficult period.

Emma began to practice the Stoic principle of differentiating between what is within her control and what is not. She realized that while she couldn't control the actions of others online, she could control her reactions to them. This understanding helped shift her focus from feeling victimized to empowering herself in the situation.

She also adopted the Stoic practice of objective judgment, where she would reframe her perception of the negative comments. Instead of viewing them as personal attacks, she saw them as reflections of the perpetrators' own struggles or insecurities. This reframing helped reduce the emotional impact these comments had on her.

Another Stoic strategy Emma employed was engaging in acts of kindness and positivity online. She focused on creating supportive and uplifting content, fostering a positive digital environment for herself and her followers. This approach not only counteracted the negativity she faced but also aligned with the Stoic virtue of contributing to the common good.

Through these Stoic practices, Emma gradually regained her confidence and peace of mind. Her experience is a powerful illustration of how Stoicism can be applied in modern digital contexts, providing practical strategies to deal with online negativity and cyberbullying. Emma's story demonstrates how ancient philosophical principles can offer solace and strength in the face of contemporary challenges.

Navigating Social Media Pressures: Overcoming Comparison and Anxiety

The story of Daniel, a college student and aspiring artist, highlights the challenges of navigating social media pressures. Like many of his peers, Daniel found himself constantly comparing his life and achievements to those he saw on social media. This comparison led to feelings of inadequacy and anxiety, impacting his mental health and creative expression.

Seeking a way to cope with these pressures, Daniel turned to Stoicism, finding in it a philosophy that emphasized inner strength and personal virtue over external validation. He began to apply Stoic principles to his social media use, particularly focusing on the concept of controlling the controllables.

Daniel started by curating his social media feeds. He unfollowed accounts that triggered negative emotions or fostered unhealthy comparisons and instead followed pages that inspired and educated him. This simple act of choosing his digital environment was a practical application of Stoic mindfulness.

He also practiced the Stoic exercise of negative visualization. Daniel would imagine how his life would be without social media and realized that many of the things he envied online were not essential to his happiness or personal growth. This practice helped him gain perspective and appreciate the real value of his life and achievements.

Another Stoic strategy Daniel embraced was focusing on his personal progress and self-improvement, rather than external accolades. He set his own standards of success, based on his values and goals, and celebrated his small victories and artistic growth.

Through these Stoic practices, Daniel learned to navigate social media with a healthier mindset. He was able to use these platforms as sources of inspiration and connection, rather than metrics for self-worth. His journey illustrates the power of Stoicism in combating the challenges of social media pressures, fostering self-acceptance, and finding contentment in one's own path.

Digital Minimalism in Practice: A Journey to Mindful Technology Use

Sarah's story is a compelling case of embracing digital minimalism, inspired by Stoic principles. As a busy software engineer and a mother of two,

Sarah found herself constantly overwhelmed by the barrage of digital information and the demands of her online presence. She felt that her time and attention were being fragmented, leading to stress and a sense of disconnection from what truly mattered in her life.

In her quest for a more balanced life, Sarah encountered the concept of digital minimalism, which resonated deeply with her. This approach, much like the Stoic philosophy, advocates for a deliberate use of technology, ensuring that each digital interaction is purposeful and enriching. Sarah began her journey towards digital minimalism by identifying what was essential in her digital life and eliminating the superfluous.

She started by decluttering her digital spaces, unsubscribing from unnecessary emails, leaving irrelevant social media groups, and uninstalling apps that didn't add value to her life. This process was guided by Stoic reflections on what was necessary for her well-being and what merely served as a distraction.

Sarah also implemented Stoic practices in her daily routine. She set specific times for checking emails and social media, creating boundaries that helped her stay present in her offline life. She prioritized face-to-face interactions with her family and colleagues, finding these to be more fulfilling and meaningful.

An essential aspect of Sarah's journey was the practice of mindfulness in her digital engagements. She became more conscious of her reasons for using technology, whether for work, connecting with loved ones, or leisure. This mindful approach prevented mindless scrolling and helped her use technology in a way that aligned with her values.

Through the application of Stoic principles and digital minimalism, Sarah was able to reclaim control over her digital life. Her story showcases the practicality of Stoicism in modern times, demonstrating how its principles can lead to a more intentional and balanced relationship with technology.

Using Technology for Personal Growth: A Path of Stoic Wisdom

Mark's story is a testament to how digital technology can be harnessed for personal growth when guided by Stoic wisdom. As a lifelong learner and a high school history teacher, Mark found himself overwhelmed by the sheer volume of educational resources available online. He wanted to use these resources to enhance his knowledge and teaching methods but often found himself lost in the vastness of the digital world.

Inspired by Stoicism, Mark began to apply its principles to his use of technology. He started by defining his purpose for using digital tools – to enrich his knowledge and to improve his teaching skills. This clear sense of purpose guided his choices and interactions online.

He practiced the Stoic virtue of wisdom in selecting digital resources. Instead of trying to consume as much information as possible, he became selective, choosing resources that were truly beneficial and aligned with his teaching goals. He focused on quality over quantity, ensuring that each digital interaction was meaningful and contributed to his growth.

Mark also incorporated the Stoic concept of reflection into his daily routine. After each online learning session, he would take time to reflect on what he had learned and how it could be applied to his teaching. This reflection helped him assimilate and integrate his new knowledge effectively.

Additionally, Mark used technology to connect with a community of like-minded educators and historians. He engaged in online forums and social media groups where he could share ideas, ask questions, and gain new perspectives. This communal learning approach was aligned with the Stoic idea of contributing to and learning from the broader community.

Through his Stoic approach to technology, Mark was able to transform his digital interactions into a pathway for personal and professional growth. His story illustrates how the principles of Stoic wisdom can be applied in the digital age to harness technology for self-improvement and life enrichment.

Lessons in Discipline and Focus

The story of Alex, who struggled with balancing work-from-home challenges and digital distractions, offers valuable lessons in discipline and focus. Analyzing his journey, we can extract practical insights and tips that can be applied to our own lives, particularly in today's digital-heavy environment.

Creating a Dedicated Workspace: One of the key strategies Alex used was establishing a dedicated workspace in his home. This physical separation between work and personal space is crucial for mental focus. It sets a clear boundary, signaling to the brain that it's time for work when in that space.

Planning and Anticipating Distractions: Alex's practice of premeditatio malorum, anticipating potential distractions, is a Stoic exercise that can be applied to any aspect of life. By foreseeing potential challenges and planning for them, we can prepare ourselves to face these distractions without being derailed.

Embracing the Stoic Focus on Control: Alex's realization that he could not eliminate distractions but could control his response to them is a fundamental Stoic teaching. Understanding and accepting what is within our control and what isn't helps reduce frustration and increases focus and productivity.

The Power of Routine: Establishing a routine, as Alex did, can be a powerful tool for maintaining discipline and focus. Routines create a sense of predictability and order, which can be particularly comforting in an environment full of uncertainties and distractions.

Utilizing Technology Mindfully: Alex's story also highlights the importance of using technology mindfully. Rather than completely shunning digital tools, which is often impractical, using them in a controlled and purposeful manner can enhance productivity.

From Alex's experience, we learn that discipline and focus in the digital age are not about drastic measures but about creating an environment and mindset conducive to productivity. His application of Stoic principles shows how ancient wisdom can be effectively used to navigate modern challenges.

Resilience in Facing Online Adversity

Emma's experience with cyberbullying and her journey to overcome it through Stoic principles provide a compelling case study on building resilience in the face of online adversity. Her story offers insightful lessons on how to apply Stoicism to modern digital challenges, particularly those that test our emotional resilience.

Focusing on What's Within Control: A key takeaway from Emma's story is the Stoic practice of focusing on what's within one's control. Emma's shift in focus from the actions of her online harassers to her reactions and internal state was pivotal in regaining her composure and resilience.

Objective Judgment and Reframing: Emma's use of objective judgment to reframe the negative comments is a classic Stoic strategy. By viewing the comments as reflections of the harassers' issues rather than as personal attacks, Emma was able to detach emotionally and respond more rationally.

Practicing Emotional Control: Emma's situation underscores the importance of controlling our emotional responses, as taught in Stoicism. Her ability to maintain composure and not react impulsively to provocation was crucial in handling the situation effectively.

Contribution to the Common Good: Despite her challenges, Emma continued to use digital platforms to spread positivity and support. This aligns with the Stoic virtue of contributing to the common good, demonstrating that one can still be a source of positivity in the face of adversity.

Seeking Support and Community: Emma's story also highlights the importance of seeking support and fostering a positive online community. Her active engagement in supportive and uplifting digital environments helped counterbalance the negativity she faced.

Emma's experience shows that resilience in the digital age, much like in Stoicism, is not about avoiding or denying adversity, but about developing the inner strength to face it head-on. Her application of Stoic principles in the context of modern digital challenges provides a blueprint for navigating online adversity with strength and composure.

Social Media and Self-Acceptance

Daniel's story of dealing with social media comparison and anxiety illustrates the challenges many face in the digital age. His journey towards self-acceptance, guided by Stoic principles, provides valuable insights into managing our relationship with social media and our self-perception.

Curating Social Media for Positivity: Daniel's proactive step of curating his social media feed to include more positive and inspiring content is a practical application of Stoic mindfulness. This act of selecting what influences our thoughts and emotions is crucial in maintaining mental well-being in a digital environment saturated with varied content.

Negative Visualization and Perspective: Daniel's practice of negative visualization, contemplating life without social media, is a Stoic exercise that helps put things in perspective. It underscores that much of what we envy or desire on social media is non-essential for our happiness and well-being.

Defining Personal Success: Daniel's shift from seeking external validation to defining his own measures of success is a profound application of Stoic philosophy. It echoes the Stoic idea of focusing on personal virtue and progress rather than external approval.

Celebrating Personal Achievements: By choosing to celebrate his own small victories and progress, Daniel aligns with the Stoic principle of focusing on self-improvement. This shift from external comparison to internal growth is key to finding contentment and self-acceptance.

Daniel's story teaches us that self-acceptance in the digital age is about understanding and redefining what truly matters. His application of Stoicism to the challenges posed by social media serves as a reminder that our worth is not determined by online perceptions but by our adherence to personal virtues and values.

Embracing Digital Minimalism: A Path to Intentional Living

Sarah's journey towards digital minimalism, inspired by Stoic principles, provides a meaningful exploration of how simplifying our digital life can lead to more intentional and fulfilling living. Her story offers an insightful analysis of the benefits of digital minimalism and practical steps to achieve it.

Identifying What's Essential: Sarah's first step in her journey was to identify what was essential in her digital life. This process mirrors the Stoic practice of distinguishing between needs and wants. By focusing on what truly adds value to her life, Sarah could eliminate the digital clutter that contributed to her stress.

Setting Boundaries: The establishment of clear boundaries around digital consumption is a vital lesson from Sarah's experience. These boundaries helped her create a balance between her online activities and her real-life responsibilities and pleasures, reflecting the Stoic virtue of moderation.

Mindfulness in Digital Interactions: Sarah's mindful approach to technology use is a key takeaway. By being more conscious of her reasons for using digital tools, she was able to engage with them in a manner that aligned with her personal goals and values, rather than out of habit or compulsion.

Benefits of a Simplified Digital Life: Sarah's experience highlights the benefits of a simplified digital life, including reduced anxiety, improved focus, and more time for meaningful activities and relationships. This aligns with the Stoic pursuit of a life that prioritizes inner peace and personal virtue over external distractions.

Practicality of Digital Minimalism: Sarah's story illustrates that digital minimalism is not about renouncing technology but about using it in a way that complements and enhances our real-life experiences. It is a practical approach to ensuring that our digital habits support our overall well-being and life goals.

In embracing digital minimalism, Sarah's story echoes the Stoic ethos of living intentionally and mindfully. Her journey provides a blueprint for how we can use technology as a tool to support our aspirations, rather than as a distraction from what truly matters.

Leveraging Technology for Growth: Harnessing Digital Resources Wisely

Mark's story of using digital technology for personal and professional growth is an inspiring example of how Stoic wisdom can be applied to make thoughtful choices in the digital world. His journey offers valuable insights into selecting and utilizing digital resources in a way that aligns with the Stoic virtues of wisdom and self-improvement.

Purposeful Selection of Digital Tools: Mark's selective approach to choosing digital resources reflects the Stoic principle of purposeful action. By choosing tools and information sources that directly contribute to his goals, Mark was able to use technology as a means to an end, rather than an end in itself.

Integrating Learning into Daily Life: The integration of online learning into his daily routine demonstrates the Stoic value of continuous growth and development. Mark's story shows how technology can be a powerful ally in personal development when used with intention and discipline.

Community Engagement for Growth: Mark's involvement in online communities for educators and historians is a modern application of the Stoic idea of learning from and contributing to the greater community. His engagement in these forums provided not only personal growth opportunities but also a chance to contribute his knowledge and skills for the benefit of others.

Mindful Consumption of Information: Mark's mindful approach to consuming digital content, focusing on quality and relevance, aligns with the Stoic practice of thoughtful consumption. This approach helped him avoid information overload and ensured that his time online was productive and enriching.

Reflective Practice for Integration: Mark's habit of reflecting on his learning and finding ways to apply it in his teaching is a Stoic exercise in practical wisdom. It demonstrates the importance of not just acquiring knowledge but also integrating it into one's life and work.

Through Mark's story, we see how digital tools, when used wisely and purposefully, can significantly enhance personal and professional growth. His approach to technology, guided by Stoic principles, serves as a model for how we can harness the power of digital resources to enrich our lives and fulfill our potential.

Conclusion: Continuing Your Stoic Journey

As you continue your journey with Stoicism, especially in the context of the digital age, enriching your understanding through various texts and books can be immensely beneficial. Stoicism, with its rich history and contemporary relevance, is well-documented in both ancient texts and modern interpretations. Here are some essential resources:

Ancient Stoic Texts:

- **"Meditations" by Marcus Aurelius:** A personal journal of the Roman Emperor, offering insights into his Stoic practice.
- **"Letters from a Stoic" by Seneca:** A collection of letters that provide practical advice on how to live in accordance with Stoic principles.
- **"Discourses and Enchiridion" by Epictetus:** Fundamental texts that lay out Epictetus's Stoic teachings, focusing on ethics and practical philosophy.

Modern Interpretations of Stoicism:

"The Obstacle Is the Way" by Ryan Holiday: A book that interprets Stoic principles for modern readers, focusing on resilience and the power of perception.

"How to Be a Stoic" by Massimo Pigliucci: An exploration of how Stoic philosophy can help navigate the challenges of modern life.

"A Guide to the Good Life: The Ancient Art of Stoic Joy" by William B. Irvine: A guide that presents Stoicism as a philosophy for attaining lasting happiness.

These resources provide a blend of historical context and modern application, offering a comprehensive understanding of Stoicism. By delving into these texts, you can deepen your knowledge of Stoic principles and their relevance in today's world, particularly in navigating the complexities of the digital age.

Online Resources and Communities

The digital world, while often a source of distraction, can also be a rich resource for learning and connecting with like-minded individuals. There are numerous online platforms, communities, and tools dedicated to Stoicism, offering a wealth of information and support for those looking to deepen their understanding and practice. Here are some notable online resources:

Online Platforms and Communities:

Stoicism Subreddit: An active community on Reddit where individuals discuss Stoic philosophy, share experiences, and seek advice.

The Daily Stoic: An online site offering daily Stoic meditations, articles, and resources. It also has an associated email newsletter that delivers Stoic wisdom to your inbox.

Stoic Week and Stoicon: Annual online events that involve a week of Stoic practices and a conference featuring talks by modern Stoic thinkers.

Digital Tools and Apps for Stoic Practice:

Stoic Meditation Apps: Apps like 'Stoic.' and 'The Stoic' provide daily meditations, exercises, and quotes to assist in practicing Stoicism.

Online Journals: Digital platforms like 'Journey' or 'Day One' can be used for reflective journaling, a key practice in Stoicism.

Podcasts on Stoicism: There are several podcasts dedicated to Stoicism, such as 'The Stoicism

On Fire' podcast, which explores Stoic philosophy and how to apply it in everyday life.

Educational Websites and Courses:

- **Modern Stoicism:** A website offering articles, courses, and resources for those interested in learning more about Stoicism.
- **Coursera and Udemy:** Online learning platforms offering courses on Stoicism and related philosophical topics, taught by university professors or experts in the field.

These online resources not only provide valuable information but also offer a sense of community and shared learning. They can be instrumental in your ongoing exploration of Stoicism, providing guidance and inspiration as you apply Stoic principles to your life, especially in the digital realm.

Integrating Stoicism into Daily Life

As you continue to explore and apply Stoicism, integrating its principles into your daily life is crucial for a sustained and meaningful practice. The essence of Stoicism is not just in understanding its theories but in living them out, especially in the face of modern challenges, including those posed by the digital world. Here are some suggestions for making Stoicism a daily practice:

Routine Reflections: Incorporate Stoic reflections into your daily routine. This could be a morning meditation on what is within your control or an evening review of your actions throughout the day. Consistent reflection helps reinforce Stoic principles in your daily actions.

Stoic Reminders: Set up reminders or prompts that bring your attention back to Stoic principles during the day. This could be through phone wallpapers, scheduled alerts, or sticky notes in your workspace. These small cues can help keep you aligned with Stoic values amidst daily activities.

Challenges as Opportunities: View everyday challenges, particularly those in the digital realm, as opportunities to practice Stoicism. Whether it's dealing with a difficult person online or managing digital distractions, use these situations to exercise virtues like patience, temperance, and resilience.

Mindful Technology Use: Practice mindfulness in your use of technology. Be conscious of why and how you are using digital tools. Aim to use technology in a way that supports your values and enhances your life, rather than detracting from it.

Community Engagement: Engage with Stoic communities, either online or locally, if available. Sharing experiences and learning from others can provide support and deepen your understanding of Stoic practices.

Continuous Learning: Keep learning about Stoicism. Whether through reading, online courses, or listening to podcasts, continued learning can provide new insights and keep your practice fresh and relevant.

Integrating Stoicism into your daily life is a journey of continuous growth and learning. By regularly practicing Stoic principles, you can develop a more balanced, resilient, and fulfilling approach to both your digital and offline life.

Overcoming Challenges and Setbacks

In your Stoic journey, encountering challenges and setbacks is inevitable, especially when applying Stoic principles to the digital age's unique complexities. These obstacles, however, are not just impediments but opportunities for growth and reaffirmation of your Stoic practice. Here's how you can use Stoicism to navigate and overcome these challenges:

Embracing Obstacles as Opportunities: Adopt the Stoic mindset of viewing obstacles as opportunities for growth. Challenges, whether in managing digital distractions or handling online negativity, test and strengthen your Stoic virtues.

Applying Stoic Flexibility: Stoicism teaches the importance of adaptability. When faced with setbacks, be flexible in your approach. If a particular strategy isn't working, be open to adjusting your methods while staying true to Stoic principles.

Focusing on Effort, Not Outcome: Concentrate on your effort and actions, which are within your control, rather than being overly fixated on the outcome, which often isn't. This focus helps maintain a sense of equanimity amidst challenges.

Learning from Setbacks: Use setbacks as learning experiences. Reflect on what these challenges teach you about your values, responses, and areas for growth. Each challenge is a lesson in disguise, helping you to become more resilient and wise.

Seeking Support and Guidance: Don't hesitate to seek support from Stoic communities or mentors when facing challenges. Sharing experiences and gaining different perspectives can provide valuable insights and encouragement.

Maintaining Consistency: Persistence is key in Stoic practice. Continue your Stoic exercises and reflections even when it seems difficult. Consistency in practice solidifies the principles and makes them a natural part of your response mechanism.

By embracing and overcoming challenges through Stoic principles, you not only grow in your practice but also deepen your understanding and appreciation of Stoicism. Each setback becomes a stepping stone towards a more resilient and virtuous life.

Continuous Growth and Learning

The journey with Stoicism is one of continuous growth and learning. As you apply Stoic principles to your life, especially in the context of the digital age, it's important to keep exploring, questioning, and evolving in your understanding and practice. Here are some ways to ensure that your journey with Stoicism remains dynamic and enriching:

Embracing Lifelong Learning: Adopt the mindset of a lifelong learner. Stoicism, like any philosophy, is vast and multi-faceted. There's always more to explore, understand, and integrate into your life. Stay curious and open to new insights and interpretations.

Reflective Practice: Make reflection a regular part of your Stoic practice. Regularly take time to contemplate how well your actions align with Stoic principles, what challenges you face in applying them, and what adjustments might be necessary.

Experimenting with Practices: Stoicism is not a one-size-fits-all philosophy. Feel free to experiment with different Stoic exercises and techniques. What works for one person might not work for another. Find practices that resonate with you and fit into your lifestyle.

Engaging with Diverse Perspectives: Seek out diverse perspectives on Stoicism. Engaging with thoughts and interpretations from different people can broaden your understanding and deepen your practice. This could be through books, online forums, or discussion groups.

Teaching and Sharing: One of the best ways to deepen your understanding of a subject is to teach it to others. Share your knowledge of Stoicism with friends or online communities. Discussing and explaining Stoic concepts can clarify your understanding and reinforce your practice.

Balancing Tradition with Modern Application: While it's important to understand the traditional roots of Stoicism, it's equally important to explore how it can be applied in the modern world, especially in relation to technology and digital living.

By committing to ongoing growth and learning in Stoicism, you ensure that your practice remains vibrant and relevant. This continuous exploration

not only enriches your own life but can also inspire
and benefit those around you in your journey
through the digital age.

"It's a funny thing, the more I Practise, the Luckier I get."
Gary Player, great golfer
1950's – 1960's

With lots of Love
from Grandma & Grandad
XXX

Printed in Great Britain
by Amazon